Three Rings and Swords-
The Bushido Code and
Stories of the Samurai

Ana Perez-Chisti, Ph.D.

ISBN # 979-8-218-03866-3

The Sufi Universal Fraternal Institute is a 501c3 non-profit organization dedicated to the study of Comparative World Religions. Classes are offered on a regular basis and open to all people for furthering understanding and respect for the many spiritual traditions. Please see the following website for more information: https://sufiuniversalfraternalinstitute.live sufimovementusa@gmail.com

<u>Gratitude</u>

To Garret Bower for his Cover Design

To the Foreword contributors: Deena Drake, 6th Dan Shidoin and Saqi Ahmed Lori Stewart, Third Dan Fukushidoin

To Robin J. Laflamme, whose photographs always captured the inimitable light.

To Kristin Fein for her serene photographs and artistry To Sensei Nancy for her Dojo photograph.

To Adam Randall for his astute perception and guiding advice.

To students in the Elder Self Defense Class who exhibited qualities of courage and perseverance that exemplified the Battle of Life.

Dedication

This book is dedicated to my Sensei's Richard Kim, Reverend Shunshin Kan and Jack Saito-san and to all Martial Artists who courageously fight the fearless battle of breaking through the boundaries of common, everyday, reactivity and arrive at the selfless Self.

practice in April of 2021, I had not regularly taught or trained in over a year.

The COVID pandemic has transformed our lives across the planet, for both good and ill. Millions have suffered and died, while others have reevaluated the meaning and purpose of their lives. Amidst this change, a renewed interest in traditional marital arts, such as Aikido has arisen. Almost every week, a new student walks through our doors looking for practice that has meaning and connects, rather than separates them from others.

Budo is defined as the "martial path or way". Early Japanese samurai were ruthless warriors who later evolved into the artists, monks, and scholars we think of today. It was their embrace of *Budo* through the daily practice of martial arts (intertwined with Zen Buddhism) that brought about this growth and change. Through daily practice and innumerable repetitions, the dedicated martial artist eventually transcends the forms and in doing so, is transformed themselves.

Perhaps it is this potential for transformation that draws people to pursue martial arts training – to transform themselves from one who reacts, to one who responds with mindfulness rather than anger. Whatever a student's motivation, Ana Perez-Chisti's writing on the ethical code of the Japanese samurai and her own transformative experiences with her martial arts teachers is particularly timely and highlights the potential value of martial arts training.

*

Offered by Saqi Ahmed Lori Stewart, M.A., Third
Dan Fukushidoin and Sufi Khalifah

In my past roles as a chaplain and as a university lecturer in religious studies, I have encountered many people who were in search of a higher meaning and purpose in life, and a spiritual

Foreward

Offered by Deena Drake, Ph.D, RN, CNS, 6th Dan,
Shidoin, Chief Instructor – San Diego Aikikai

When I first started training in the martial art of Aikido in the mid- 1990's, dojos were full of energetic, and eager students in their early-to-mid twenties. A handful of those students, myself included, went on to become teachers after training rigorously for many years. By the time I was ready to become a chief instructor in 2008, the popularity of Aikido had already been on a steady decline for several years, eclipsed by the competitive fighting sports of Brazilian Jiu-Jitsu and MMA.

By the time the COVID pandemic struck in the beginning of 2020, a good number of the Aikido dojos in the United States were in dire straits, with an average membership of 10 students, most of whom were in their 40's. COVID lockdowns closed, either temporarily or permanently, martial arts schools across the country. Rather than stopping classes entirely, my dojo moved to outdoor training in a park three times a week.

Due to my work as a Palliative Care Advanced Practice Nurse in a hospital hard hit by COVID, I was unable to commit to a regular teaching schedule and had to rely on my senior students to keep the dojo running and the community together. By the time vaccinations were readily available and we returned to indoor

Foreward

Offered by Deena Drake, Ph.D, RN, CNS, 6th Dan,
Shidoin, Chief Instructor – San Diego Aikikai

When I first started training in the martial art of Aikido in the mid- 1990's, dojos were full of energetic, and eager students in their early-to-mid twenties. A handful of those students, myself included, went on to become teachers after training rigorously for many years. By the time I was ready to become a chief instructor in 2008, the popularity of Aikido had already been on a steady decline for several years, eclipsed by the competitive fighting sports of Brazilian Jiu-Jitsu and MMA.

By the time the COVID pandemic struck in the beginning of 2020, a good number of the Aikido dojos in the United States were in dire straits, with an average membership of 10 students, most of whom were in their 40's. COVID lockdowns closed, either temporarily or permanently, martial arts schools across the country. Rather than stopping classes entirely, my dojo moved to outdoor training in a park three times a week.

Due to my work as a Palliative Care Advanced Practice Nurse in a hospital hard hit by COVID, I was unable to commit to a regular teaching schedule and had to rely on my senior students to keep the dojo running and the community together. By the time vaccinations were readily available and we returned to indoor practice in April of 2021, I had not regularly taught or trained in over a year.

The COVID pandemic has transformed our lives across the planet, for both good and ill. Millions have suffered and died, while others have reevaluated the meaning and purpose of their lives. Amidst this change, a renewed interest in traditional marital arts, such as Aikido has arisen. Almost every week, a new student walks through our doors looking for practice that has meaning and connects, rather than separates them from others.

Budo is defined as the "martial path or way". Early Japanese samurai were ruthless warriors who later evolved into the artists, monks, and scholars we think of today. It was their embrace of *Budo* through the daily practice of martial arts (intertwined with Zen Buddhism) that brought about this growth and change. Through daily practice and innumerable repetitions, the dedicated martial artist eventually transcends the forms and in doing so, is transformed themselves.

Perhaps it is this potential for transformation that draws people to pursue martial arts training – to transform themselves from one who reacts, to one who responds with mindfulness rather than anger. Whatever a student's motivation, Ana Perez-Chisti's writing on the ethical code of the Japanese samurai and her own transformative experiences with her martial arts teachers is particularly timely and highlights the potential value of martial arts training.

*

Offered by Saqi Ahmed Lori Stewart, M.A., Third Dan Fukushidoin and Sufi Khalifah

In my past roles as a chaplain and as a university lecturer in religious studies, I have encountered many people who were in search of a higher meaning and purpose in life, and a spiritual

Contents

Sensei Richard Kim

*

<u>Preface:</u>

Learning the Martial Arts as a life training is experienced everyday in all circumstances. Every moment in life is a chance to awaken to the great Bushido Code, which is to treat all beings with respect so there is no inclination to cause harm within ones self or in ones surrounding environment. However, it must be stated that self-defense is a guardian of truth and when applied without hatred or vengeance, a way opens for greater expansion of consciousness. The following experience unfolded in my life while being a student of the Martial Arts and it was the motivation that inspired me to write this book on the **Three Rings and Swords: The Bushido Code and Stories of the Samurai.**

I was walking with my friend up on the hills in Berkeley to observe the sun set during one beautiful fall evening. Trees and dense forest surrounded the path. We wanted to hike out to a point in the hills where one could see the full vista of the Oakland/San Francisco panorama. We arrived at a beautiful meadow that was open from any obstructions providing a wide vista. It was a clear evening and the lights on the bridges and buildings began to twinkle. We sat in the grass gazing at the scene for longer than expected and then began to walk the four miles back to our car in the dark. My friend rushed ahead of me. I thought he might want to relieve himself on an abiding tree and he did not want me to see him so I just took his decision easily without any question. I walked by myself for about a mile and began to get concerned about him.

Then out of dense set of trees, a person jumped out at me as though in full attack to harm me. It was at that moment my instinct and Martial Arts training reasserted my muscular memory and I moved my arm immediately in place to block the attack. My strength of motion came up from a deep well of remembrance and the force of my defensive move was powerful. When the man landed on the ground screaming in pain, I looked down at the broken nose on the face of my friend.

"What do you think you were doing?" I asked in surprise. "I was only trying to play a joke on you," he said while blood was oozing down his face. *"Never do that again or frighten anyone for some kind of joke. To frighten someone, as you have found out, you injure yourself,"* was my retort as I helped him up and walked him back to the car.

After getting my friend to the hospital to reset his broken nose, I realized the depth of importance of Martial Arts training. To use one's martial training to defend against a perpetration of one's safety is a valuable tool in life and the training remains always in one's muscular memory. But anyone repeating the traumatization of what one would ignorantly consider, *"a joke,"* or any action that would cause harm to another either by way of instilling fear or violence of any kind is a violation and sacrifice of the collective well being of humanity. A Martial Artist does everything they can to avoid harming another as will be evident in the stories that follow.

This simple occurrence with my friend gave me the reason why I, as a woman Martial Artist, wanted to write the stories that reveal the training of the Bushido Code and of the many different warriors who exemplified the life of the Samurai. For these chosen beings, unusual circumstances arose under unexpected conditions activated by the political powers of the time. As they placed enlightened warriorship before their consciousness, they lived as examples of their training, discipline, fearlessness, and their awakened condition of *"mushin"* (empty mind). The Samurai's actions became the foundations for moral philosophy. It is through the three Sensei's, mentioned below, who exemplified the practices of the great Samurai, that the Bushido Code of true warriorship would reach around the world.

*

About the three Sensei's

Sensei Richard Kim

The following selections of stories are taken from the classes I attended with Sensei Richard Kim from the Zen Bei Butoku-Kai in San Francisco, California during the years between 1969, 1971 through 1975. These stories are all extracted from my notes that I took during his classes. If there are any errors in the transcription of the historic stories, these are my errors and I take full responsibility for them. His teachings and lectures about the history of Okinawan and Japanese grand masters offer an invaluable perspective about the inner integrity of the Samurai, and the Bushido Code. Sensei Kim studied with many great Sensei's such as Kaneko-sensei, Arakaki, Taoist priest Chao Hsu Lai and Gogen Yamaguchi and his line of stories reflect their teachings. May these stories open the door of awareness to all students at the Shorinjiryu Kenpo school that teaches one how to be a true spiritual warrior through meeting the greatest test…. mastering oneself.

Sensei Reverend Shunshin Kan

Added stories and experiences come from my Kendo and Iaido studies during the 1960's with Reverend Shunshin Kan who was the pastor at the Buddhist Church in New York City on Riverside Drive and 105ᵗʰ Street. He was the founder of the Ken-Zen Institute on 26th Street in Manhattan until his death in 1987. The Ken Zen Institute is a Japanese cultural and martial arts center attracting many students from around the world. Reverend Kan was a well-educated man with a master's degree in literature and a Ph.D. in Indian Philosophy. He was a Zen practitioner who taught thousands of students to take on the discipline of Kendo/Iaido (Art of the *Sword Kata*) and to live by the Truth that leads a student to their Origin. He was trained as a Zen Buddhist practitioner coming from a long line of Buddhist Masters.

Sensei Jack Seito-san

I have also included stories from Jack Seito-san beloved Sensei and friend whose humility and kindness resides in my heart. He was an example of an authentic noble spirit and a "perfect gentleman". His legacy was transmitted in the simple tasks of service to others that awakened the consciousness so that it might be illuminated. He continually reminded me of the inner work that was necessary to fulfill the vocation of a Master searching for the Origins of Truth through the Zen way of empty mind and no fear of death (*Mushin*). He was a trustworthy practitioner of

Bushido, a meditation master and a disciplined *Kata* practitioner. It was in an international guesthouse in San Francisco where we were both employed and in Golden Gate Park where he offered his greatest teachings to my future husband, Robin J. Laflamme and me. Yet, his compassionate and unflappable manner remains impressed in my being as the stories below will indicate.

Sensei's Kim, Kan and Saito have been the epitome of spiritual warriorship and excellence, exhorting me to go further and further than they did. Their respect of me as a woman studying the Martial Arts was honorable and deeply supportive as all three Sensei's recognition was focused on the wholeness of a person, their many dimensions and most importantly their spiritual evolution. I have only veneration and great gratitude for their training, their wisdom and for being holders of the Bushido Code. I sincerely hope your life will be enriched by their amazing stories and experiences as mine was.

Ana Perez-Chisti Orinda, California

*

A Short History of the Samurai

In the 12th Century the samurai were considered aristocratic warriors or "*Bushi*". They rose to power in the Meiji Restoration in Japan around 1869 due to their warrior skills and disciplined training. They often studied Zen Buddhism and were known to influence the artistic and cultural development of Japan particularly during the Muromachi period (1338-1573) by creating the tea ceremony, cultivating beauty through flower arranging, calligraphy and poetry. Most schools that trained the Samurai exposed a code of conduct formulized as Bushido, which stressed courage, bravery, honor and personal loyalty above life itself. The virtues of politeness, fidelity, justice, humility, purity and mercy prevailed under the Tokugawa period (1603-1867). The act of *seppuku* (disembowelment) was respected as an alternative to any level of defeat. Although the Samurai were a small group during Tokugawa period they stabilized society by becoming artisans tradesmen, bureaucrats and military leaders. They were allowed to carry the double sword as a code of honor and peace prevailed for over 250 years until the Western powers took action against the Tokugawa regime in the early 19th Century.

It is interesting to note that the term *"Bushido"* was not used until the 16th Century and only in the Kamakura period (1192-1333) did the term begin to surface. Zen Buddhism, Taoism, and Confucian thought including disciplined training and frugal living as well as devotion to the emperor became a major obligation and duty. The title, *"perfect gentlemen"* was the code that exemplified the Samurai.

Kendo was a fencing form of disciplined training using swords made of bamboo called a *"Shinai"*. In the modern century, since the government disallowed actual sword combat, the study of Kendo with the bamboo sword became a means for cultivating discipline, patience and a method for building character. Practice armour was designed to protect the body, arms and head from harsh strikes that caused injury. Today, many students worldwide practice the art of Kendo and participate in matches organized by the Kendo Federation formed in 1970. Contemporary Sensei's today use Kendo skills as a means to redirect students into higher ethical behavior, insight and personal discipline.

*

Lineage of the Zen Bei Butoku-Kai in the USA

Many of the stories that follow in this book are extracted from Sensei Richard Kim's teachings. To clarify the philosophy and structure of the Zen Bei Butoku Kai, I offer a short summary of the basic viewpoint given to all his students, which I am honored to say, I was one of them.

The lineage of the Zen Bei Butoku Kai in the USA is organized as a flat structure with various dojo instructors having almost complete autonomy as the final authority and responsibility comes from the Dai Nippon Butoku Kai. There is no line structure like the military where each level controls the lower and then requires the lower level to answer to the higher level. The flat structure is democratic in nature. The only safety to insure the lineage teachings stay in tact is by the instructor's character and integrity.

The practice and dedication of the Martial Artist is a long path up the mountain if mastering the art of *"mushin"* (empty mind) is desired. If a practitioner only gets part way at least the by-product is a good self-defense tool. It is understood that there are many ways up the mountain: Yoga, Zen, Kendo, Sufism and other Martial Arts techniques: Pa Kua, Aikido, etc. But in the lineage of the Zen Bei Butoku Kai the quickest path is learning to control the breath, pure concentration, meditation and the performing of *Kata,* which prepares one to face any difficulty in life.

The top of the mountain is Satori (enlightenment or *Kensho*), which is an awareness of reality by knowing yourself. Ordinary reality is seen through the filter of the intellect, which imparts limited interpretation on it and shades or filters consciousness. As long as the intellect dominates the Martial Artist can never see the true reality because of the filter effect unless you reach Satori. Satori (*Kensho*) is the absence of intellect. Therefore to reach *Kensho,* a Martial Artist must do away with the intellect, which means a "Zen Death". The intellect will fight you all the way because intellectualization is an ingrained process.

The dividing line between the finite world and the infinite world represents the breaking down of the intellect that in its essence represents a death. It is a breaking point that will become stuck before one is able to cross to another level. An analogy is running: when you get tired, if you continue running without stopping, you reach a second wind, and you will then feel as if you can run all day. When you cross the dividing line, you will see logic in what was before illogical. Everything will make sense and your body and mind will unite as one. This text reveals those master Martial Artists who achieved breakthrough and who brought the living legacy of Bushido to the world.

CHAPTER ONE

The Bushido Code

No Parents, only heaven and earth
No Home, only the base of the spine
No Life or Death, only the breath
No Laws, only adaptation
No Principles, only self No Talent, only wit
No Sword, only *Mushin*

Knowing that human beings at the base of their nature have uncontained possibilities toward violence, the Samurai meet these impulses with tranquil stealth. Their actions are mediated internally from deep practice of calm mind in exceptional circumstances; whereas common attractions for wealth and power hypnotize the majority by activating imaginings of the four enemies: control over others, shame, fear or blame and can lead many to misguided actions.

Those who are trained in the Bushido Code know the impermanence of these illusionary states and choose instead to fight the enemy within themselves. The enemies are dangerous and always lurking in the corners of the human habitat. Therefore the great battle is to first fight the enemies within and then, if one encounters them from outer circumstances, a method of sure victory will be the achievement gained and that comes when no injury activated by control, shame, fear or blame touches another or oneself. This is why the Bushido Code is practiced.

There are three approaches within Martial Arts training that can be assessed when working with a skilled teacher. I call these approaches: **Three Rings and Swords.** The "Swords" represents an aspect of the Samurai's training that slices through ignorance and entanglements, here in this text it alludes to the necessary internal and intuitive training which helps guide an aspiring student to a level of *satori* (enlightenment) and truth. Each of the three "Rings" represents the external form of training. Qualities like faithfulness and discipline that arises from a symbol of devotion and acceptance through the treasure of one's teacher (referred in this text as one's Sensei). The symbol of the Ring is a promise one gives to a power greater than oneself toward the unbroken continuity of spirit. This awareness only occurs when the student's evolution is ready for the inner battle.

Three Rings and Swords

The First Ring-TRUTH---The First Sword-the VOW
The Second Ring-ETHICS---The Second Sword -INSIGHT
The Third Ring -TRAINING---The Third Sword -COURAGE

*

The First Ring-TRUTH

With the risk of a student getting carelessly caught in the evolution of their ego, the teacher is needed to guide and expose the student to The First Ring-Truth. The student's responsibility is to move steadily toward receptivity to the teacher. This state will bring the student to The First Sword-the Vow, which will be explained below.

Naturally all students come to a master with many levels of consciousness and limitations induced from ignorance in their upbringing or trauma that had not been worked through psychologically. The teacher might even appear in simple garb or in a humble profession. The development of a student's inner understanding is based on whether or not they can understand the reason for their experiences such as one might find in Zen studies. As Miyamoto Musashi's Guide explains, *"The samurai and Zen went hand in hand...and it aimed directly at the true nature of things. There are no ceremonies, no teachings: the prize of Zen is essentially personal Enlightenment, which does not mean a change in behavior but realization of the nature of ordinary life. The end point is the beginning, and the great virtue is simplicity."*[1]

It is here in the Zen principle of simplicity and a constant willingness to learn from experiences in life, a truth that is exemplified by this teaching story that was shared in Sensei Richard Kim's class about a Samurai and a simple fisherman.

*

The Samurai and the Simple Fisherman:

During the Satsuma occupation of Okinawa, a Japanese Samurai, who had lent money to a fisherman, made a trip on collection day to Itoman Province where the fisherman lived. Unable to pay the debt he owed, the poor fisherman fled and tried to hide from the Samurai, who was famous for his short temper when dealing with unethical behavior. The Samurai went to the fisherman's home and, not locating him there, made a search of the town. As his search for the fisherman proved fruitless, the Samurai grew furious. Finally, at twilight, he came across the fisherman cowering under an overhanging cliff. In slowness, he drew his sword. *"What do you have to say?"* he shouted.

The fisherman replied, *"Before you kill me, I want to make a statement. Can you grant me this humble request?"* The Samurai responded, *"You ingrate! I lent you money when you needed it and also gave you a year to pay, and this is how you repay me. Out with it, before I change my mind."*

"I am sorry," the fisherman said. *"What I want to say is this. I have just started to learn the art of the empty hand and the first thing I learned was the precept: 'If your hand goes forth, without your temper; your temper goes forth without your hand.'* The Samurai was astonished to hear this from the lips of a simple fisherman. He put his sword back into its scabbard and said, *"Well, you are right. But remember this, I shall be back one year from today, and you had better have the money ready."* Thereupon, he left.

Night had fallen when the Samurai returned home and, as was the custom, he was ready to announce his return when he noticed a shaft of light streaming from his bedroom through the door, which was slightly ajar. He peered intently from where he stood and could see his wife sleeping and the faint outline of someone sleeping next to her. He was startled and exploded in doubt as he realized it was a Samurai as the person was wearing the special robe of the Samurai.

He drew his sword and stealthily crept towards the room. He lifted his sword and was ready to charge into the room when the words of the fisherman came to him. *"If your hand goes forth without your temper, your temper goes forth without your hand."*

He withdrew his sword and went back to the entrance and said in a loud voice, *"I have returned."* His wife got up, opened the door and came out with his mother to greet him. His mother had his clothing on. She had put on his Samurai clothing to frighten away intruders in his absence.

The year passed quickly and, come collection day, the Samurai made the long trip again. The fisherman was waiting for him. As the Samurai approached his home, the fisherman ran out and said. *"I had a good year. Here is what I owe you and interest besides. I don't know how to thank you."* The Samurai put his hand on the fisherman's shoulder and said, *"Keep the money. You do not owe me anything, I owe you. You taught me a lesson*

I should have remembered from the days when I was learning to be a Samurai." He revealed to the fisherman what had happened and the story spread. After this story became known, the villagers and the fishermen pooled together their resources and built what is now known as the White God Temple in Itoman, Okinawa were many people now travel and pray. [i]

In the ancient tradition around the 12th Century of the Japanese Samurai, war and destabilization of the empire was constant. The Bushido Code was a natural development of the feudal code of ethics that integrated Shinto and Confucian ideals such as loyalty to the ruling emperor, honor of one's ancestors, and filial piety. It was also a time when Buddhism came into religious dominance and brought the ideas of stoic composure when under duress of any kind. There was a code of honor for those Samurai that aligned within the various schools of martial training and as political pressure would have it, often these schools became adversarial causing argument and conflict regarding methods of training.

But the worldly principle found in Confucianism indicated that all beings are fundamentally good. In The Bushido Code, the Samurai endeavored to train themselves to recognize that goodness exists in all beings and situations so that cultivated approaches to the world that reflect respect for people motivated their actions. Often, their approaches reflected those virtues found in Confucian thought. Their interaction would exhibit benevolence, wisdom, propriety, justice and fidelity. Although the Samurai were constantly tested by competing groups who were under the guidance of different teachers, the many Samurai followed close to the Confucian principles as stated by the philosopher Tsang who said, *"I daily examine myself on three points; --whether in transacting business for others, I may have been not faithful; --whether, in intercourse with friends, I may have been not sincere; --whether I may have not mastered and practiced the instructions of my teacher." [ii]*

The Samurai had a desire for ethical education such as that found in seeking justice inclusively when necessary. The virtue of justice was philosophically presented to the community by Confucius to function and to keep each person in the place that they were destined to fulfill and there-by serve the harmony of the whole. There was no guarantee that the general will of the people or the Emperor's who were in political power at the time would be just, but that ethical ideal is the reason the Samurai always trained to improve themselves, perfect their faults and self-create a higher level of humanness.

This was not an easy task under the circumstances of a warring society. Yet even so, the Samurai had to find methods of true selflessness, in which the doer cannot be present any longer as an individuated person. Only the spirit is present, a kind of awareness, which shows no trace of ego. [iii]

The principles of enlightened Warriorship were based on living their lives in dedication of conquering self-doubt, aggressiveness and negative behavior. They sought wisdom by accessing a deep well of insight born from meditative and difficult physical endurance practices. They also learned from nature as Lao-tzu, the Tao and his meditative teachings were highly esteemed.

Most certainly, there were those bad eggs that wanted to show off their skill as swordsman and kill with impunity. Often times, a Shogun (governor of a prefecture) would petition a match between competing Samurai by betting money on one or the other opponents or exposing a ribald clan who sought out fame. It was a common occurrence the Samurai faced. This was often found as the reason they retreated into the mountains to get away from these situations. They did not leave because they feared encounters or challenges. They left for moral reasons knowing they would win in many of these competitions, and the death of the young opponent would be the outcome. The Samurai had great skill in sensing the inner development of the challenger by observing the level of their *"ki"* (the inner energy force) and by the strategy of their physical moves. Their decision to fight another was often decided from the state of deep awareness as most had reached *Kensho (*enlightenmen*t).*

In synchronizing mind and body the Samurai found self-mastery that awakened inner transformation. This spiritual pathway opened inwardly to them as they began to respect the natural ways of being. If the Samurai survived the perils of their time, they walked directly into the unbroken Truth, the Origin of their being and they arose as Masters who set the illuminated selfless state of being as the goal of their discipline and were responsible for seeding the stages of the Bushido Code within the Martial Arts legacy.

(Photograph by Kristin Fein)

The First Sword - the VOW

A vow is a solemn promise or assertion, one by which a person binds him/herself to an act, service or condition.

When one works with a *Sensei* (teacher), an inward movement is initiated; a door that seems closed becomes opened. The Samurai in training all knew this code and sought out the best teachers they could find in their areas or else they travelled far and wide to be tested and shaped into the masters they knew they could be.

The *Sensei* pursues the inward movement and, without influencing the course of development helps the student in the most secret and intimate way he or she knows; by direct transference of the spirit, as it is called in Buddhism. *"Just as one uses a burning candle to light others with,"* so the *Sensei* transfers the spirit of the right art from heart to heart, that it may be illuminated. If such should be granted to the student, he/she remembers that more important than all outward works, however attractive, is the inward work which one has to accomplish if one is to absorb the vocation of a true Samurai.[iv]

This transference of inner awakening is detailed in the story of Odagiri Ichiun who lived between 1619-1706. These dates are approximate as many great Samurai and their histories where not fully recorded in the principle archives of the Province in which they lived.

*

Odagiri Ichiun and Three Conditions

Odagiri would teach children about the efficacy of *yin* (feminine) and *yang* (masculine) and how they must know about masculinity but prefer femininity. A young swordsman was passing by and heard him speaking to the children and said, "*What nonsense is this? I heard that you said that everyone must have this kind of awareness but I believe in technical excellence which is performed by my good right arm.*" The swordsman asked for a lesson from Odagiri about the feminine way. Although Odagiri did not have a sword he found a piece of toilet tissue, rolled it up into a long tube and decided to use it as his weapon. The swordsman was infuriated by this act of disrespect because he thought Odagiri was making fun of him. The swordsman threatened an attack and Odagiri just sidestepped him and pushed the toilet paper tube up the swordsman's nose. Because Odagiri had attained *Satori*(enlightenment), he perceived what the swordsman was thinking showing him that he was going to cut Odagiri in the head, after this move. But just as the mental thought arose in the swordsman Odagiri told him, "*If he had a sword instead of toilet tissue tube, you, (the swordsman) would be dead.*" The

swordsman understood at that moment Odagiri's meaning of knowing masculinity but preferring femininity. [v]
This story designs for the Martial Artist the expanded training of the Samurai and the methods that were used to develop mastery.

Odagiri taught his students three conditions for becoming a true swordsman.

1. **Know the condition of the your opponent.**
2. **Know yourself.**
3. **Develop your perception.**
   These conditions are elaborated
   below with the following stories.

1) To Know the Condition of one's opponent:

Sensei Kim's honored the Samurai Odagiri Ichiun above many others because he practiced the Sword Kata every day of his life. Although he looked like a modern day hippie, he never cut his hair or shaved and he always wore old worn out clothing and lived under a bridge where people of dangerous character congregated, he always felt inclined to live near those who struggled for existence at he gained greater purpose and insight into reading people. He sought neither fame nor fortune because he believed that it would engulf him and cause him to lose himself. He always sought the quiet meditative state. Because of his dedicated awareness, he developed a method of reading the minds of his opponents. Due to his intuitive awareness, he could tell when an adversary was thinking of making a certain move in the type of sword attack. For example, when the opponent was thinking of striking his head with the sword, Odagiri responded, *"When you hit my head, I will strike your side"*. The opponent became so alarmed he thought he would trick Odagiri. The opponent thought, *"I will fake a strike to the head but hit his hand instead"*. Odagiri responded, *"As soon as you hit my hand, I will strike your throat."* The opponent realized no matter what he did, Odagiri would read his thoughts and he was powerless against him. When the match occurred between the two men, the opponent lost.

Odagiri felt the *Kata* is similar to a Mantra. The repetition of defined movements allows one to release thoughts and merge into a calm, clear state of consciousness that only can be attained after thousands of repetitions.

In the first phase, when a student studies Mantra, or a sacred phrase given to them by their teacher, the student responds to the request of the teacher to recite the Mantra out of respect for the teacher's request. It is the same as a *Sensei* who is requesting students to practice *Kata*.

The second phase of the recitation as well as the *Kata* movement brings often a question as to what the teacher wants by the repetition.

The third phase is how the student reacts after thousands of repetitions and who anticipates his teacher's call by acknowledging the deeper meaning hidden in the repetition. This stage often progresses the student into equality with the teacher or shows a superior attitude.

A Kendo analogy would be something like this: The *Sensei* strikes and the student blocks—the student blocks without thinking; the second time, the *Sensei* strikes and the student blocks—the student thinks to him/herself that maybe there is another way to block and he/she is thinking of other things besides doing the block; and the third time, the teacher strikes and the student blocks—he/she had done it so many times that they block automatically without thinking, so that now one is free to look around and anticipate a strike.

Odagiri's student's always asked him if he could anticipate all his opponents' attacks? He told them, if they wanted to test him at any time in his life whether he was awake or sleeping, eating or whatever, that they could attempt an attack. They never succeeded. [vi]

*

Hariya Sekiun (d. 1662)

Odagiri's great master *Sensei* was Hariya Sekiun who trained 2800 students during his lifetime of which Odagiri was his most prized pupil as he had received the *Inka* (the pure transmission). Odagiri also wrote everything down so that Hariya's teaching would not be lost. Much of the Samurai legacy of teaching was done through aural transmission and not written down.

Hariya was a model of The Bushido Code and accomplished master of his time. Between the ages of 65-70, he engaged in 52 matches to the death. Every single one of these matches he encountered the champions of the many different schools and he won every match without killing one person.

Odagiri approached Hariya, who was then 70 years old, and asked him why he had not killed anyone in the matches. Hariya showed Odagiri his blunted sword as his secret. His inner power was so great, and depending on the severity of the attack, he only broke an arm or knocked the opponent on the head, which made them go unconscious. Although Hariya desired to teach rather than kill any opponent, there were those that insisted he fight them to the death as the story below indicates.

*

Hariya and the Person with the Helmet

To show how skillful Hariya was, one day a person came to him and said, *"I have heard that you can kill a person with a slow stroke of your wooden sword even if the person is wearing a metal helmet."*

Hariya said that it was only a story but the person insisted by bating Hariya with the fact that he had this new metal helmet that would protect him from a head blow. Hariya then asked if the person was married and did he say farewell to his wife today. The person laughed and replied, that he had the best metal helmet that money could buy and he was confident that Hariya was just any old man who could not harm him with a simple wooden sword. Hariya hit him right on the helmet with a slow stroke as if he were in practice and the person was knocked backwards so hard, he hit against a tree and fell over dead. It was a terrifying demonstration that was witnessed by Odagiri and Kohaku, the Zen monk. Hariya did not want to do it but when the person insisted his fate was sealed.

*

East and West-A perspective

Knowing how to act from the highest purpose of one's being so that outward confirmation of inner events can proceed from a place of equanimity is a product of dedicated training. From the point of view of my *Sensei's,* the basic difference between East and West is that Eastern practitioners use intuition and Western practitioners use intellectualization. The Western person has also developed an anthropomorphic God while the Eastern person feels the basic harmony in the universal structure of reality but is always aware of an ever-present opposing faction.

The Western person leans into postulation or facts that are found through science or those studies that are intellectually directed which is outside of the intuitive ways of knowing. Therefore in the East, there is a great impulse in the student to find a master who can teach the inner ways of knowing. In the West, a student is less inclined to seek out those who are wise and knowledgeable about the intuitive ways of knowing and thus the Eastern impulse to find a master with these inner developed methods is a gift to the Western student as they search to develop their unique innate abilities.

For a student of the Martial Arts, following a *Sensei* is essential. A student's training is analogous to a military search squad crossing a minefield. The first person that makes it across leaves footprints so that the others can follow. If the others do exactly as the first person, they will make it across without harm. If anyone of the persons goes their own way, they take a chance of stepping on a mine and getting blown to pieces.

In the West, the motion of the individual soul is a powerful concept. In the East, this is not so important. Eastern traditions bring one to emptiness, and boundlessness. Western traditions lead the individual to a universal pattern of concern, work, study, and creativity. Because there are many more cultural freedoms and patterns in the Western traditions there are many more possibilities given to the individual whose basic potential is to experience all these dimensions so that one's soul has the capacity to transform anything it comes into contact with. In Eastern philosophical thinking it directs one to boundlessness. The individual is not seen as a unique universal idea that transforms reality but a part of the greater whole that is constantly progressing toward an ultimate and dynamic unity.

In the West, a student wants to say, *"I want to discover my own path."* But the intellectual person who comes to a *Sensei* to receive teaching and yet who is not empty enough to receive the basic intuitive teaching that is necessary for skill in the Martial Arts, is like overflowing bowls of tea as the following story shows.

*

The Student, the Sensei and Tea

A student wanted to learn from a *Sensei* but instead of absorbing the teachings reflectively, the student kept asking the *Sensei* many questions. The student wanted to learn about Zen but every time the *Sensei* tried to explain something, the student would interrupt the *Sensei*. Finally, the *Sensei* seeing the problem decided to serve tea. When Sensei poured the tea into the cup, the tea filled to the brim and he kept pouring until it flooded onto the floor. The student became perplexed by the *Sensei's* action and asked why the *Sensei* kept pouring the tea? The *Sensei* replied, that the student was like the cup—so full of his own ideas, he had no room for anything else.

2) To Know Oneself:

To know oneself means to gain insight into the nature of one's ego. The motivation of the greatest of masters was that of humility. So many influences that come to a person can test whether or not the ego has developed and evolved past the need of finding recognition in the eyes of the world. It requires thinking beyond our immediate surroundings, never being off duty regardless of what role we chose to play in life. The way to know oneself is by sharpening our instincts so that one can navigate through difficulties and ego entrapments. This story that follows indicates how a very famous master of the Martial Arts evaded even the great Emperor of China because he shunned recognition and honoring that the Emperor wanted to give him as he considered it an entrapment

*

The Master of Great Humility

It is not unusual that one can find great masters living in run down areas of villages around the world. One day, the Great Emperor of China sent his Prime Minister out to find a famous master of the Martial Arts because he publically wanted to give him awards in front of many of the townspeople and dignitaries of his court. To the shock of the Prime Minister, the address that he was given was in the worst crime infested neighborhood. The Prime Minister thought there must have been a terrible mistake, as a master of such expertise would not want to live in such dilapidated conditions. But since it was the only address he had, he finally found the exact shabby house and saw a man in front of the house pulling weeds and doing manual labor in the garden area. The Prime Minister asked the workman if the Master was home. The laborer asked the Minister why the Master was being sought. The Prime Minister said that the Emperor wanted to give the Master all the fame and recognition that he deserved because of his legendary skill and was going to put on a huge event for the occasion.

The workman replied, *"Oh, Well….when he comes back, I will be sure to tell him the good news. I think he will return tomorrow morning."*

The Prime Minister was delighted to hear this information and gave a special written invitation for the Master saying to the laborer, *"Will you please give him this invitation and address which will gain him entry into the palace and also that he might gain audience with the Emperor".*

When the Prime Minister returned to the palace, the Emperor asked him if he was successful in the finding the Master. He responded by saying he did not find the Master as the workman told him he will return in the morning. I gave the invitation to the workman who was working in the garden. When the Emperor asked the Prime Minister to describe the workman, the description enraged the Emperor. " *You stupid fool, that was him. Go back and grab him tomorrow and bring here to me immediately.*" When the Prime Minister went back to the run down house, the Master was gone. [vii]

To know oneself a student must activate great patience, as a student one must realize learning takes time. Building outer and inner skills necessary to fulfill one's true capacity in any field of endeavor requires a willingness to be trained in the disciplines of self-control. This is articulated in the story of the student Matajuro who went to his *Sensei,* Bonzo for training.

Matajuro asked Bonzo, "*You are very famous swordsman, so tell me, what if I train everyday, seven days a week, from the time I wake up to the time I sleep, how long will it take me to become a master?*" "Ten years," said Bonzo. "*What if I train twice as hard?*" asked Matajuro. "*Thirty years,*" replied Bonzo. "*I don't get it,*" retorted Matajuro. "*You told me if I train hard, it will take ten years but if I train twice as hard, it will take me thirty years?*" "*I don't understand,*" said Matajuro. "*Well then, I will tell you, it will take seventy years,*" said Bonzo.

Matajuro was exasperated by this time and thought to himself, "*First he says ten years, then when I say I will train twice as hard, he says thirty years and when I question him, he tells me seventy years. I will never be a master*". The great *Sensei* Bonzo reading his student's mind said, "*The person who is in a hurry will never learn.*" Eventually, Matajuro did learn and became a very great swordsman. [viii]

*

Understanding KATA

The *Kata* (a soft form) in itself is a teacher forever. One does not have to go to a dojo except to be under the skillful eye of a *Sensei* whose function is to see that one is going in the right direction. The achievement of self-perfection is more important to the Martial Artist who possesses it than his physical and technical ability. *Kata* takes great faith, tenacity and hard work to master. Every time one practices the *Kata,* his or her first move and his and her last move remind them of the ancient saying brought by Gichin Funakoshi (1871-1957) who brought moral philosophy into the Martial Arts said, *"karate ni sente nashi"*. It is stressed incessantly throughout all Bushido training, *"In karate, there is no advantage in the first attack."*[ix]

In the moral philosophy that Funakoshi brought to karate he changed the pedantic external movements of what was found in jujitsu as simple street fighting to the power of a *karateka's* (student practitioner) inner state and one who never strikes first, and never strikes in anger. He brought attention to the *Kata* that always began and ended with a defensive movement and this repeats what Samurai learned from the fisherman, *"If your hand goes forth, hold back your anger; if your anger goes forth, hold back your hand."*

Therefore, training oneself in the *Kata* (soft form) allows the meditative and physical being to unite within oneself before any action is taken externally. Actually *Kata* is a form of a Koan, which is a verbal problem that cannot be solved intellectually as one has to go beyond the bonds of rational thinking. *Kata* is a Japanese word meaning *"form"*. It is similar to a moving Koan. It refers to the detailed and choreographed patterns of Martial Art movements practiced alone. *Kata* can also be practiced in groups when training in unison. *Kata* is most often used in Japanese and Okinawan martial arts such as in Iaido, Kendo, Kempo, Karate and Aikido although in Aikido *Kata* often a partner is included in the practice.

Kata develops the essential characteristics of concentration, balance and breath control. The different *Katas* that the master's transmitted to their students were detailed and choreographed flowing movements that developed the mind as they had within these movements defensive strategies to strengthen the memory.

As *Kata* is performed in a tranquil state of inner imagination, it prepares the student for any action that might arise from an external physical aggression. The *Kata* teaches one not to rely simply on force to protect oneself (or others) but serene quiet of the mind while in the multiple functions of physical actions, imagination, and breath control. The outcome brings balance and many aspects of one's being are assimilated into these carefully designed movements.

When the student finds out that *Kata* gives a separate reality beyond the senses, when he/she discovers the real secret behind the *Kata/Koan* which the teacher would never be able explain to the karateka, (Martial Arts student), then their world will stop as they know it and they will see themselves as they really are and they will see as their *Sensei* sees them. The *Sensei* can never give the student enlightenment; he/she can only show you how to get there if they have already been there.

Kata also helps tune a karateka's body mechanics such as muscular memory needed to execute Martial Arts techniques properly. *Kata* works by harmonizing the *yin* (passive, feminine, cool, dark) and *yang* (active, masculine, heated, bright) energies.[x] The discipline of the *Kata* is devised in such a way that when a student perfects it, there forms in the person a perfect equilibrium between physical and mental aspects of oneself. In other words, one reaches a state of *Satori* (enlightenment).

Knowledge of *Kata* is essential to understanding how to generate strength from the core as opposed to just using the legs and arms. In *Kata* every pore of the body is awakened and the karateka gains control over the external actions. In the *Kata,* a prescribed set of movements and patterns are memorized by the karatekas especially for the purpose of defending oneself against attackers. A student learns to face the fearlessness of death through these contemplative movements and an absolute control of the breath is necessary when dedicating oneself to *Kata* practice.

In many of the *Kata* forms, the master Martial Art *Sensei* creates different methods and movements. There were many *Katas* created by different masters showing a depiction of a mock fight as defensive drills or a set of rules that were created to allow the *Kata* to fit the training sequence. In that no written transmissions of these methods were exchanged between *Sensei* and student, the basic form had to be memorized the same way as dancers memorize movements in ballet. The benefit that arises from sincere *Kata* practice is found in the story about Terada Soyu.

*

Terada Soyu

In the story of Terada Soyu (d. 1825) at the age of 82 years, it is said he was an exemplary Samurai because he could read the minds of his opponents. When anyone wanted to make a move to strike him during a match, he would call out their move and tell them what they were planning to do very similar to Odagiri Ichiun. His method always put his opponent off base because he was always correct.

He developed this insightful capacity through the diligent practice of *Kata*. *"The Martial Artist trains so he/she can stand alone. One dies alone as no one dies with you. If one knows they can face death emotionally (not intellectually), one can read the opponent's mind."* Terada believed that a Martial Artist could never reach inner perception unless they were able to face death.

Practicing *Kata,* Terada indicated, requires no special form for the practitioner but rather a dedicated mind where one can feel as if it were the last move one makes on earth. One accepts their death and makes up their mind that the block one used will destroy the aggressive action of the opponent. If a practitioner does *Kata* practice in such a manner, the secret of the *Kata* will be revealed and a critical zone around the body will be magnetized.

As Gichin Funakoshi who was well known for his mastery in *Kata* said, *"That if you master the Kata, you don't need self-defense because it's all in the Kata. With Kata you will get to the point where you will be able to intercept (anticipate) your opponent's moves. Kata will let you conquer fear and transcend yourself by becoming egoless. All that is necessary is one Kata, but you must practice it constantly until you "break out".*

*

Funakoshi and Three Attackers

Because Funakoshi was very famous, there was always great jealousy among many men who wanted to prove themselves against his mastery. They took the unfortunate risk of attempting to attack him for no reason but only to prove to their ego that they were better fighters. There is a story of Funakoshi who was walking on a road to another village while being followed by three men who wanted to attack him to prove how skillful they were. Two men had weapons, a *Sai* (a three-pronged dagger similar to a hairpin blade with two claw-like pieces on either side. This is a traditional Okinawan Melee Weapon). The second man was carrying a *Bo* (a long wooden staff) and the third man was empty handed. Funakoshi used his *"Ki"* (inner power from the solar plexus, called *Manipura* in Sanskrit) to jump into a nearby tree and waited until the man with the *Sai* was in correct location for him to act in a defensive move. Funakoshi then jumped out of the tree landing on top of his attacker breaking his neck and picking up his *Sai* threw it into the chest of the attacker holding the *Bo*, the third attacker seeing this situation, ran away. Funakoshi's move happened in a flash of a second and became legendary in the Martial Arts that supported the validity of *Kata* as a perfected form of inner training.

*

Understanding "Ki"

"Ki" is universal energy, which is activated, in our human form. *"Anything that has form must have a beginning. For example the sun is said to be blazing now, but there must have been a beginning to the fire. There must also have been a before, before the fire started. If we trace the origin of all things, we reach a point at which nothing existed. On the other hand, nothing cannot give birth to something. Therefore in the Orient the word "Ki" applies to the state, which is also the real nature of the universal. Pursuing this condition even farther we find a point at which the sun, the stars, the earth, humans, animals, plants, water, air, everything is the same thing. "Ki" has no beginning and no end; its absolute value neither increases nor decreases. We are one with the universal and our lives are part of the life of the universal.*[xi]

3) Develop your perception:

Development of perception is an important step in the student's evolution. There are several forces that are very powerful and the first is willpower. An individual usually runs this power until they hit a block in the road where it no longer takes them forward through the will. They realize there is something else that must carry them and that is the perceptive power within one's consciousness that arises when the energetic systems are relaxed, peaceful and the *"Ki"* is free. The story below of Kyan Chotoku gives evidence to this awareness.

*

Experiences of Kyan Chotoku

Although Kyan Chotoku was very diminutive in stature, 5'2", he could send down his *"Ki"* (central solar plexus canal of golden yellow light energy) to the depths of the earth and was immoveable. His ability later became an important practice for his students in the Martial Arts and many masters of *Tai Chi* and *Pa Kua* could extend their *"Ki"* like roots 12 to 18 inches into the earth. The more relaxed a practitioner is the less one thinks of their strength as only muscular as no tension is there to block the *"Ki"*. Tension is caused by stress and that indicates there is fear in the mental realm. Stress makes one feel anxious and muscles will tighten.

Sensei Kim mentioned a story about monks from the Nakano Spy School. Practicing monks would walk in circles many times repetitively until even if there is slight air current when walking, the monk will feel it. This exercise enables one to feel the environment around oneself and become very sensitive to any form of vibration.

These monk practitioners became so sensitive that they can tell whether or not the floor has been swept recently without ever looking before stepping down upon it. They developed a physical/psychic acuteness with everything that is considered outside themselves—within their environment. This is part of the Oriental Philosophical training where one masters everything outside oneself after mastering that which arises from within ones being.

Therefore, Kyan believed that a person should practice *"Seisan"*, (the soft form of *Tai Chi*). He practiced this soft form for seven years. Kyan had a theory that if he was completely relaxed with his *"Ki"* fully circulating, it could explode in forward or backward motion that could elevate him with the blast of sudden noise. He would ask one of his students to make a sudden noise while he was close to an object in a room such as a table or chair. When the noise blast occurred, Kyan would leap many feet into the air and land on the top of the object. It is said, he also did this from a boat and landed on a bridge above. What was unusual about Kyan's practice is that he could jump backwards as well as forward and this was believed to be extraordinary.

The story of Kyan's springing into a sudden jump shows the value of the *Kata* (the soft form). The *Kata* aids every movement as all movement comes from the *tanden* (*Manipura-* Sanskrit) chakra at the solar plexus). When one is standing still, the practitioner tries to bring their mind down to the *tanden* and experience an unobstructed concentration. At first this takes mental effort but soon becomes automatic and then any movement one makes is the *tanden* making it.

Perception such as this extends into all movements with the sword as extended *"Ki"*, the *tanden* is advancing or retreating. Soon the swordsperson will realize it is not the body alone but the *tanden* that is making the hands, feet and sword move. That is what is meant when one hears the terms, *"Soft-style vs. Hard-style"* practice.

The so called internal system offered by Kyan was the inner code of complete relaxation with soft style verses that of hard style, e.g., pushing, throwing, blocking, etc. Actually, this might be a case of terminology only as soft and hard style might be the same thing when examining each method deeply. [xii]

In Miyamoto Musashi's Book of the Void, he says, *"To attain the Way of strategy, as a warrior you must study fully other martial arts and not deviate a little from the way of the warrior. With your spirit settled, accumulate practice day-by-day, and hour-by-hour. Polish the twofold spirit heart and mind, and sharpen the twofold gaze perception and sight. When your spirit is not in the least clouded, when the clouds of bewilderment clear away, there is the true void."* [xiii]

Integration in one's training is absolutely necessary to attain mastery. *Sensei* Kim always began each class with *"pushing hands"*. He indicated we were not pushing with our hands but rather with our *tanden* and the *tanden* was dispersing energy into our limbs. If we are blocking an action, the tanden is blocking as the hands and legs are only appendages of the *tanden* moving in our bodies. He emphasized that we must practice in this way. We then were led into practice of *Tai Chi Chuan, Pa Kua* and other *Kata* forms.

To recap therefore, the First Sword-The Vow means to hold priority over one's developing perceptions and remain faithful to the practice and discipline that is necessary to accomplish one's ideals. As one holds inner resolve steady, self-cultivation and self-creation will bring forward The Bushido Code that will guide and support wisdom to flourish in the world. Moral excellence, love and all virtues bring the highest possible attainment to any Martial Artist.

CHAPTER TWO

The Second Ring – ETHICS

Ethics is the investigation of sources, principles, sanctions and ideals of human conduct and the development of character. Ethics have opened multiple areas of investigation into psychological, practical, evolutionary and theoretical evolution of the human from the earliest generations of society. It brings to our consciousness the investigation of right and wrong in human sentiment, the capacity for judgement and relationship to virtues that dictate conscience. The well-being of the community at large has always been a primary tenet developed by reflective thinking people. In modern society, *"do no harm,"* is the clarion call for the virtuous. Therefore a practice of mental control when dealing with any form of ignorance, hatred or violence was necessary. Decisions that were made from a calm mind are a discipline of Zen Buddhist practice. The Samurai realized that all action was cultivated within through internalizing Zen discipline and the study of Confucian thought and the Tao.

Zen Buddhism can be traced back to Myoan Eisai from the 12th Century who brought Zen practice to Japan after visiting China. Bodhidharma brought Zen Buddhism to China in the 6th Century CE called *"Ch'an Buddhism."* Inclusively, the Analects of Confucius approximately written between 551-479 BCE became the impulse for deeper reflection on the Bushido Code in China and Japan. The Samurai were familiar with the teachings of the Confucius who guided one from accumulating blame and who advised the following behavior, *"Hear much and put aside the point of which you stand in doubt, while you speak cautiously at the same time of the others, then you will afford few occasions for blame. See much and put aside the things, which seem perilous, while you are cautious at the same time in carrying the others into practice, then you will have few occasions for repentance. When one gives few occasions for blame in his words and few occasions for repentance in his conduct, he is in the way to get emolument."* ("emolument" meaning...the individual is on the right path.) [xiv]

The attitude of mental and physical training by the Samurai and the ethical use of the sword became strongly ingrained in the very sinew of the Japanese people down to the modern era. Life was frugal and not easy for anyone, but the warmth of spiritual training was there. Honor and consideration concerning false pride were abandoned. Rather the Samurai embraced the truth, in singleness of thought and practice until they found that there is neither self nor other, that the general mass of common everyday people and those that thought themselves more worthy are of one essence. The Samurai firmly held on to this belief and never moved away from that unified awareness. The Samurai were not slaves to words or dictates or bound to conceptual discrimination. Their training was to maintain an inner ethical serenity and all actions moved from that state of knowing.

Few people realize today that the Samurai did not always draw a sword to quell a disturbance or to restore peace. It is quite true that the Samurai regarded their two swords as symbols of their soul, an esteemed property. But most importantly, they regarded the loss of consciousness or any misguided actions that brought shame as an essential reflection of their morality as their honor was dearer than life itself. There was many times in the Samurai's daily work that situations would develop, and their very presence would be considered so strong that their long sword would not be drawn to testify to their strength and skill. Perhaps here, at this moment, one can observe the Samurai's belief that says, *"If your mind is clean and orderly, you will make your environment clean and orderly too."* [xv]

*

The Samurai and the Toothpick

The Samurai's ethical code kept them frugal in all manner of life. They would not take food from those who had little although it was offered with complete generosity by their hosts. When the Samurai knew the hardship of others, they would not act in such a way as to make it more stressful for those that generously offered the little they had. For the Samurai, to know and to act are one and the same. One can see paintings of Samurai with toothpicks in their mouths indicating to the hosts that they were well fed and had already eaten so that the hosts would not be embarrassed or upset by the Samurai's refusal to take food that was genuinely offered. The code to help others always guided the Samurai into selfless behavior even though they might be starving. Battling hunger was one of the important methods the Samurai used to train themselves, as they knew that the one who conquers him/herself is the greatest warrior.

*

Avoiding an Altercation

If someone of unequal skill tried to threaten a Samurai or attack them, they would do everything in their power to avoid an altercation. They were inwardly astute to look for the right way that brought the virtuous code of behavior to light. They sought education and travelled widely remaining in constant movement to seek knowledge and greater understanding. They were aware that a guide to this knowledge was a precious gift and they often sought out master teachers who could help them polish, correct and evaluate their skill. While moving from village to village in search of new experiences and wisdom, they cultivated their patience, endurance and simplicity by being an example to all those they met as they became living examples of the Bushido Code. They worked at different jobs and had many skills that improved the community life. They often worked in menial jobs, which helped them integrate into the community seamlessly so that they could cull out the danger that lurked under the malice of prejudice.

Ethics as the major essence of the Bushido Code is highly communal and calls out instinctively an obligation to all Martial Artists by revealing the method of how the disposition of virtues resides within the individual practitioner. There is no possibility in the training of any Martial Artist that this First Sword-The Vow can by bypassed and neglected.

(Sensei Kan and Ana Perez-Chisti)

The Second Sword-INSIGHT

Insight is the power of apprehending the inner nature of reality. A Martial Artist trains so they can stand-alone with the intuitive nature of seeing all circumstances. To fully absorb and accept the integrity of one's evolution, regardless of how humble the exhibiting characteristics of the moment, it is as a maturation and inner development that is necessary for all who wish to walk this path. Unless one can develop the inner nature of reality and to face death, a person never develops extraordinary perception where one will be able to effectively read on opponent's intentions. The following story of Terada Soyu gives evidence to this awareness.

*

The Historic Match with Terada Soyu

Terada Soyu was a master of perception. He had a sparring match set up to test whether his old school style of *Kata* training (soft style) where one activates alone using physical movements while contemplating defensive methods verses the new sparring style with an opponent using a *shinai* (split bamboo sword) paired in a championship match.

The tournament was arranged between the two schools of training. Terada was a participant and represented the "old school". He felt that *Kata* training was sufficient to prepare for a match to the death with the masters of the *shinai* sword or "new school" of training.

The contestants were divided into two lines with "old school" on one side and "new school" on the other. The first match that was called into the center playing field was Terada and he was to face the champion of the new school. The new school participants all thought, *"Just wait until this guy faces a man whose shinai (bamboo sword) has become part of him and then Terada will see the flames of his opponent's "Ki" shoot out through his shinai."*

(Chiba Shusaku who was about 20 years old at the time recorded the following account of this historic match. The account of the match is a direct translation.)

The contestants were divided into two lines with the old school on one side and the new school on the other. First to fight was Terada and he was to face the champion of the new school. The others were paired off down the line and were to fight after Terada. Some of the others from the old school were worried. Terada was offered protective gear to wear but he refused saying that, " *I have never used that so I don't want it now but you can use all your want.*" Following his lead, all members of the old school copied his decision and also refused protection. Terada was in his late 60's or early 70's at this time.

When the champion and Terada finally faced each other for the match, the champion thought to himself, "*Well, he's just an old man so I won't hurt him. I'll just tap him on the head,*" But Terada told him after he had thought that, "*I know what you are thinking, you think I am an old man. Well the moment you strike for my head, I will break your arm.*" This is exactly the counter for this kind of attack.

Terada had spoken these words out loud so everyone could hear them. The champion grew alarmed at the idea that Terada could read his mind so he decided to attack with a fake to the head first, then suddenly switch and strike Terada's side. Right after he thought that, Terada said aloud again, "*When you attempt to hit my side, I will poke your throat.*" Now the champion knew Terada could perceive his intentions, so he dropped his *shinai*. Terada won the match without throwing a strike. It was the same with all the others trained in the old school.

Chiba wrote in his diary, "I spoke to all the players from the new school. They all said, "*When I saw Terada in action, I realized the value of the old school Kata style, before I though it old fashioned. He changed my thinking.*"[xvi]

As the legacy of soft style *Kata* training developed so did the artistry of the Samurai. The Samurai became important contributors to the culture of their time and advanced the ethics of community well being. The stories below reflect their contribution as well as their masterful and insightful development.

(Photo by Robin J. Laflamme)

*

Yagyu, Yoshioku, Musashi and the cut flower

Many Samurai were known to have artistic development in calligraphy, painting, and the tea ceremony as well as in *Ikebana* (flower arranging). Their artistic methods are still present today in many aspects of Ikebana practice and training. Yagyu was known for his perfect mastery in flower arranging and in the components of combining natural elements such as rocks, sticks, leaves, flowers and moss, and he showed his artistic awareness through symmetry. While he was working on a special arrangement, a threat came to his dwelling from a member of the Yoshioka clan who wanted him to come to a dual with their leader, Yoshioka. Instead of using his sword and taking the dual, he cut one of the flowers with his sword and asked his maid to deliver it to Yoshioka.

When Yoshioka received the flower, he became enraged and threw the flower on the floor of the inn where he had taken up residence with the one intention to fight Yagyu. He stalked out past the maid enraged and angry. The maid picked up the flower and admiring its elegant beauty took it back to Yagyu's courtyard and planted it once again.

When Miyomotu Musashi, one of the great Samurai of all time, walked by the garden and saw the flower, he knew that a master swordsman had cut it, because when Yagyu had cut it, he had put his *"Ki"* into his sword, and when the flower grew again, there was a special aura corresponding to the place where it had been cut and Musashi perceived that perfected energy in the aura. Yoshioku had failed to recognize this level of inner mastery or the significance of Yagyu's perceptive development.

Sometime later, Musashi was visiting the inn again and saw the flower still living in Yagyu's courtyard. Having recognized the unusual aura on the flower, he did not know that Yagyu was still living there. Musashi attempted to duplicate the cut but no matter how he tried, he could not do it. He finally decided he would give the flower the best cut he was capable of giving and leave it at that.

He called the maid and asked her to kindly deliver the flower back to the person who originally cut it. When she brought the flower back to Yagyu, he held it in his hands and asked the maid, who was the person who gave this flower to her. She replied that it was Miyomoto Musashi. It was at that moment that Yagyu knew the clan of the Yoshiokas was defeated. [xvii]

CHAPTER THREE

The Third Ring-Training

Training is designed to lead one to some result in some orderly succession of circumstances. Zen Buddhism, Taoism, Confucian philosophy sets East Asian Martial Arts apart from the training of the Martial Artist in the West. Meditation techniques have a strong emphasis on the mental discipline of the Martial Artist as well as their spiritual development. As the Samurai mastered the different meditation techniques and brought about the state where the rationalizing of the mind came into coordination with the action of the body, the intuitive nature excelled. The Samurai could respond immediately to the changing situation around them and act from a state of calm awareness. These philosophical principles of mental tranquility, fearlessness, and spontaneous responsiveness to all occurrences were central to training in Zen and Taoism.

Zen did not develop fully in Japan until the 12th Century. Zen teaches that the Buddha-nature, which lives in all beings, can bring one into *Satori* (enlightenment). The only limitation in which the Buddha- nature lays dormant is due to one's ignorance. A path of training was opened up for the student to awaken not only by the study of Sacred Texts, or ceremonial rituals but also by disciplined practice that dislodged the common thoughts of the rambling mind. Thus, meditation and contemplative practices were enhanced with different martial techniques for the physical body.

"Self-awareness cannot be solved by logic; you must find the answer through meditation. Meditation is not just Zazen, which is only a small part. Zazen, formal sitting, will give you proper posture, breath, and steadiness of the mind and so is indispensable but still it is only a part of the meditation. You can find Samadhi...complete equilibrium...only in Zazen. The rest of your meditation must be informal...when you eat, you eat; when you sleep, you sleep. You must get to the point in your training at which you are doing informal meditation twenty four hours a day."[xviii]

Buddha discovered *Nirvana,* a state of joy where there is neither death nor rebirth. Nirvana is different from *Satori* (enlightenment). *Satori* is the fully awakened mind and heart in life but *Nirvana* is getting off the wheel of rebirth. Buddha achieved *Nirvana* and also discovered *Karma,* the law of cause and effect, of action and reaction; it is a natural law, which has nothing to do with the idea of justice or reward and punishment. He said, *" Until you reach Nirvana you would continually be reborn."* He found that life is suffering and pain brought on by desire and this places one on a constant rotating wheel of suffering, old age, sickness and death. He advocated that one must overcome desire in order to get off the wheel of constant return.

Buddha said to his disciples, *"What we call life, as we have so often repeated, is the combination of the Five Aggregates, a combination of physical and mental energies. These are constantly changing; they do not remain the same for two consecutive moments. Every moment they are born and they die. When the Aggregates arise, decay and die, 'O Bhikkhu, every moment you are born, decay and die. Thus even now during this lifetime, every moment we are born and die, but we continue. If we can understand that in this life we can continue without a permanent, unchanging substance like Self or Soul, why can't we understand that those forces themselves can continue without a Self or Soul behind them after the non-functioning of the body?"* [xix] The only way to do that is through individual awakening, the knowledge that everyone is capable of finding inside oneself *Satori* (enlightenment). This short story of the two students gives insight to finding one's way and their own willingness to accept training.

*

The Two Students

Two students who were friends were studying at a monastery to become monks, as they wanted to reach enlightenment. The abbot felt that one of them had reached the point at which he would benefit by studying with another master abbot and so told him to take a trip. As he was packing, his friend asked if he might go along with him. When the student who was leaving asked why his friend wanted to accompany him, his friend replied…"*So I can learn from you*". The monk who was leaving told his friend, "*When I eat, it will not satisfy you; when I sleep it will not give you rest; when I study it will not build your knowledge.*" A teacher can show you the way but they cannot give it to you or do it for you.[xx]

The best practice to find one's inner state is through meditation and one must do it all the time by oneself. Ones state of mind is based on ones endeavor to connect meditative practice to true ethical behavior which is found in the Seven Mindfulness practices given by the Buddha to his adherents: **Mindfulness, Investigation of the Dharma, Effort, Rapture, Tranquility, Concentration and Equanimity.**

Mindfulness can be considered as a 'form of recollection" but is more accurately symbolized as a gate-keeper whose joy is to keep eyes on the people passing in and out, restricting entry to only proper beings. Mindfulness is a major factor toward the development of ethics, and oversees our duties, guards and educates us. It also reminds us to open the door to the good and restrains the negative. Furthermore, it reminds us to keep continual vigilant attention on our duties preventing negligence.

Investigation of the Dharma is the encouragement to study the work and writings of those masters of wisdom that have raised their lives and minds to higher levels of meritorious actions. Studying of the Dharma gives release to the Law of Dharma to flourish and blossom and thus leads one to liberation and freedom, transcendent of rebirth and cravings that bind us to continual suffering.

Effort is one of the three central and important factors around which all the other factors revolve. The Buddha says: *"Striving should be done by yourselves, the Tathagatas (the enlightened ones), are only teachers"*. The effort to avoid arising unwholesome thoughts means that the practitioner is advised not to cling to an after-image and its activating details but rather to practice composure over the faculty of sight and other senses. How a person deals with all arising sensations of the mind with detachment is the key to maintain effort.

Rapture (Joy) is an intense appreciation held mindfully on what one is practicing. This is an important aspect for training as it is connected to the Four Immeasurable: Loving kindness, Compassion, Appreciative joy and Equanimity. These build expansive perseverance and inspiration for the Martial Artist to continue in one's endeavors.

Tranquility arises when concerted effort is achieved in all actions.

Equanimity is different from tranquility in the sense that it directs one to maintaining a balance in mind and body. The consciousness is no longer disturbed by conflicts, fears, sadness and desires. The ultimate goal is attained as indicated by the Buddha who says to his disciples:

Through many a birth in existence wandered I,
seeking, but not finding, the builder of this house.
Sorrowful is repeated birth.
O house-builder (craving), thou art seen. Thou shalt
build no house (body) again. All Thy rafters (passions)
are broken. Thy ridgepole (ignorance) is shattered.
Mind attains the Unconditioned (Nirvana).
Achieved is the End of Craving.[xxi]

*

Meditation Exercises

Meditation exercises are available through the many contemplative traditions such as Zen and Buddhist practice. Following is a simple exercise that reflected Jack Seito-san's approach that was very helpful to me. When one starts their meditation session, first close your eyes but not fully shut. This helps the student sense seclusion from the sensual stimulation of seeing outer objects. Cast the gaze slightly downward at a specific spot. When sound distracts the mind, the instruction is to let the sound be there by itself, without thinking about whether one likes the sound or not. Simply let the sound go and let go of the mental fist around the sound. Relax the tightness in the head, feel the mind become calm and at ease. Redirect the attention back to the object of meditation, the breath. Relax the tightness in the head on the out-breath, feel the mind become open, peaceful and calm. One stays with the breath and relaxes the tension in the mind until the next distraction appears by itself.

One does this with all senses, smelling, tasting, bodily sensations, and thoughts of any kind of distraction that pulls the mind away from the breath. Whenever there is a distraction of the sense doors, one must let it go, relax that mental fist around the distraction and loosen the tightness in the head. Open and expand the mind and redirect the attention back to the breath again. It does not matter how many times the distractions arise. One simply allows these distractions to be there every time any of the senses arise... just remember to let it go...loosen the tightness in the head, feel the mind expand and come back to the breath.

Sensei Kim often suggested after the meditation practice was finished that one press the palms of their hands together, like at the end of a soft form *Kata*. This is necessary because of the large electric currents going through the body that were produced by the meditation exercise. Next, he advised we go into a shoulder stand, as taught in Yoga, for about ten minutes, followed by the cobra stretch for the back and then the corpse position where one lays flat on the back with arms stretch out 90 degrees from the body. Be completely relaxed as possible. Run the mind down throughout the body to check that all the muscles have been relaxed. Then hold this corpse position for about 10 minutes or until the body feels completely rejuvenated.

*

Jack Seito-san and the young man

Jack and I worked together at the same hotel in San Francisco. Jack Seito-san was born in Hokkaido, Japan and he was a master of meditation and a *Sensei* of the many Martial Art forms and a particular master of *Kata*. His inner state was unflappable. Every action and humble job he did at the Majestic International Hotel was done with grace and ease and quietude. Jack (he always wished to be called by his first name) was in charge of all levels of domestic housekeeping and I was the night clerk at the front desk. Often we would talk and spend time in conversation while everyone slept. I would often follow him in his *Kata* practice, which he did regularly without fail. I would watch him as he did his tasks and he was careful, mindful and precise in all he did. Every time Jack touched anything, it was left in an immaculate condition. He seemed to have this touch that turned everything into a jewel of precision and beauty.

One night I remember Jack was cleaning up in the main waiting room in the lobby. A young blond haired man came into the lobby from being out at a saloon, as he was pretty inebriated and hostile. Jack saw him but did not pay much attention to him, or so I thought. I tried to figure out whether or not I was going to call the police to come and help if the young man acted out in any way. I knew Jack was present if anything happened unexpectedly.

The young man was loud and looking for trouble. He called out to Jack with racial slurs but Jack continued his job cleaning without reaction. When Jack did not react to the young man's provocation, the young man picked up a glass ashtray and threw it at Jack's head. Without even turning around, Jack moved slightly to the right and the ashtray passed his head and smashed on the floor.

Completely calm, Jack turned around and came over to the young man who was much bigger than Jack and stood in front of him with the most penetrating gaze I have ever seen. Very slowly, Jack reached his hand out to the young man's shoulder and he said, *"It must be very hard to bare when someone you care about very much leaves you."* The young man stood there in the moment shocked into immobility. Within an instant he fell into Jack's arms sobbing.

To my observation, the young man had already been in a fight as his faced was bruised and so were his hands. He was fairly worked up emotionally before the encounter with Jack but after Jack's comment, things changed rapidly. I brought the young man some coffee and toast and the three of us sat awhile together in the lobby not talking but being present with each other.

Dawn was rising and my replacement was about to arrive for the morning shift. Jack suggested the three of us take a trip to Golden Gate Park before people woke up so we could be in the beauty of the park without the disturbances of external energies. We caught the bus and proceeded to head to the park walking pretty much in silence. Jack found a beautiful spot under the trees and we sat down on the grass. Jack asked the young man to tell us about his affair and about his life. After we sat and listened to his story, a calmness and renewed silence came between us again. Jack asked us then to simply listen to the wind, the leaves on the trees and the grasses, the birds, and the small sounds of bustling people awakening and moving about. He told the young man to watch his breath as did I and soon we were absorbed in a blissful peacefulness.

We remained in that united, silent space for a while, I did not really know the exact amount of time that had passed but I felt rejuvenated. The young man was now completely sober and his disposition was changed into this articulate, kind fellow. When we started to leave, he was very grateful to Jack and me and asked Jack if he could see him again. Jack courteously accepted but asked the young man to consider studying meditation and the Martial Arts.

Jack knew of a Zendo (a school for Zen study) where the young man could begin his training. He also said, *"If you sit in Nature everyday and simply listen and watch your breathing, much will be revealed to you."*

I saw the young man several times after that first encounter. He and Jack would go off together for a period of time. I could not accompany them on these trips as I had to work but I perceived a deep change in the young man's personality. His charming qualities began to shine out and there was more consideration in his communication. Jack effortlessly went back to doing his humble tasks as housekeeper, the way he always did but after this incident, I knew without a shadow of a doubt that I was fortunate to be with a true Sensei of the Bushido Code and a master of meditation and *Kata*.

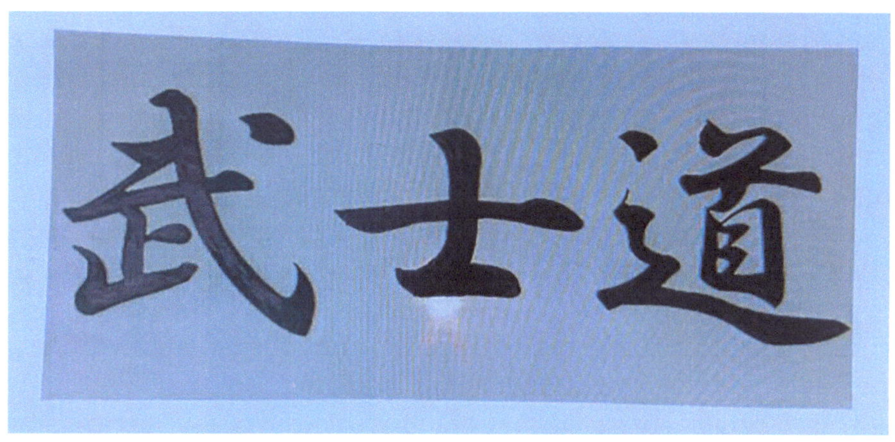

The Third Sword-COURAGE

Courage is a quality of mind that meets danger or opposition with intrepidity, calmness and firmness. Courage has two sides: one of moral courage and the other as physical courage. Moral courage, which takes greater strength, is that quality that enables one to pursue a course deemed right through which one may incur contempt, disapproval, or opprobrium such as being disgraced in society. Physical courage depends on bodily strength and fearlessness.

Reverend Kan's life story, which I remember him telling us in a Japanese Restaurant, as we shared bottles of Saki, was an example of fearlessness and great courage. As a young boy of 17 years old, he was conscripted along with thousands of teenagers into the *Yokaren* (Japanese Navy), considered an elite group and quickly trained to become a pilot. His mission was to fly his plane into an American war ship that was guarding the Pearl Harbor Coast of Oahu, Hawaii. The flight was a *Kamikaze* mission (suicide mission) as the boys were tasked to give their lives in a last ditch effort toward the end of the WW II.

These brave young men were celebrated as Cherry Blossoms, a flower that had a short existence; they would fall from the tree in full bloom and gave off a radiant color. These flowers became their symbol and was often embossed into the buttons of their uniforms, and also embroidered by their family members into scarves and tokens that the pilot carried with them for the mission in which their lives would fall as the blossoms from the tree.

Reverend Kan took his mission and flew out one early dawn. Over the Pacific well before he reached his destination, a US War Ship shot him down. Although his plane went down, he managed to survive and was retrieved from the water by the Navy crew who brought him abroad and placed him in containment on the ship.

To Reverend Kan's surprise, he was treated with great respect. It was during this time on the ship while in deep meditation; he realized he was going to offer his lineage training of the Samurai Bushido Code to Americans from that point on and give back to those in the Western world, that knowledge that was transferred to him by his elders and master teachers. He always shared his feelings about the honor and nobility of the American soldier and held great respect for all those who encounter unacceptable circumstances.

"Every Master who practices an art molded by Zen is like a flash of lightening from the cloud of all-encompassing Truth. This Truth is present in the free movement of his spirit, and he meets it again, in "It," as his own original and nameless essence. He meets this essence over and over again as his own being's utmost possibilities, so that the Truth assumes for him—and for others through him—a thousand shapes and forms." xxii

To meet one's destiny without complaint but rather with interest in the adventure changes how the path of a life will unfold. Courage is necessary to meet the circumstances without fear that one will fail. All experiences that the Samurai met were portions of their own being reflected through the circumstances of their lives.

According to the principles of Buddhism, if a person is to develop well there needs to be an equality of characteristics that benefit himself/herself and those are compassion and wisdom. Compassion represents love, generosity, kindness, tolerance, and reflects from the heart of a human being, while wisdom would reflect the qualities of the intellect and the mind. Both qualities are equally needed in the Martial Artist. But what we find in Sensei Kan's story is a very young conscripted *Kamikaze* pilot and his willingness to promote honorable obedience aiming at a mandate induced per the political climate of the time. From the political powers that were in control, killing and destroying the enemy by sending young men to their inevitable death and by sacrificing their lives was considered a contribution to the Emperor and the county.

The Japanese government recognized the army as an extension of the National Police Force during the 1940's, which had broad implications regarding foreign invasion, security of the homeland, and any defense policies necessary to protect the people. The Japanese soldier felt that war means a minimal if not a committed level of self-defense, which was a National requirement of every conscripted soldier.

Although Reverend Kan was educated in the wisdom tradition of Zen discipline and philosophy from an early age, he felt obliged to follow with courage the intention of the moment to protect the National interests and the people and stay true to his *Sensei's* training and remain fearless by doing so. Reverend Kan's perspectives about these times in his youth were transmitted to his students usually in a relaxed manner while having sushi in a café and sharing convivial conversation. Reverend Kan did not abandon his promise to his Mother Country but he also found reconciliation with his new country, the United States of America.

There are evident challenges that test a practicing Martial Artist whether it is following the laws of the land where one is born or abide by the high standard of honor that develops in relationship with other nations and particularly with one's teacher.

As one progresses, there are different degrees of courage that a student of the Martial Arts might be tested and that is shown in their resolve to hold their relationship with their *Sensei* in high esteem even when the experience of the relationship seems weakened by circumstance. The story of Nakayama and his student Murakami shows this teaching well.

*

Nakayama and Murakami

Nakayama was a fine *Sensei* of the Butoku-kai and leading instructor of the *naginata* (spear--a curved blade at the end of a long shaft). Nakayama was well off financially and could support the school where he taught. He had a devoted student named Murakami who became like a son to him. It so happened that Murakami's mother was injured during WWII in an air raid strike by a bomb blast and Murakami had to take care of her and the medical bills mounted. He became destitute with nowhere to turn. He shared his condition with his friend who suggested he go to his *Sensei* and asks him for financial assistance to cover the bills.

Murakami explained the situation to Nakayama who very generously accepted to help Murakami but under several conditions that must be met. Nakayama indicated that Murakami pay 10% interest each month and if he missed a payment he must pay an extra 20%. This request made Murakami very angry but he did not show his reaction to his *Sensei* but kept his feelings inside. When Murakami told his friend what happened, the friend said that Nakayama was rotten to the core and that Murakami should leave him immediately and search for another *Sensei*.

After some contemplation knowing that he wanted to help his mother, he said he would pay Nakayama back no matter what the debt may be. It took Murakami many years to repay the debt and by this time Nakayama was very poor as he continually used his resources to support the Martial Arts school.

After Murakami had paid the final installment of his debt, he was ready to leave Nakayama's school as his student. Nakayama asked him to wait before he left and presented him with a bank note. The sum interest deposited that was collected from Murakami original loan had grown quite a bit over the years. Murakami had realized in that moment that he had misjudged his *Sensei* and tears of gratitude and remorse came to his eyes. [xxiii]

It takes great courage, insight and discipline to trust in one's ability to ride out the many unexpected relational experiences that come to a person during their lives. To see beyond the circumstances that one is experiencing without judgement of someone else, takes a certain kind of training that causes one to reflect inwardly so that the inner eye is awakened to meet the circumstances with a new creative possibility. It is what Murakami was being taught by his *Sensei* Nakayama when he was given back the Bank Note to his loan.

"The courageous person is one who always keeps their presence of mind, so far as a human being is able. So though one will fear those fearful things, they will endure them as they should for the sake of that which is noble, for this is the aim of virtue."[xxiv]

In the Buddha Dharma, the combination of the Five Aggregates (that which compose a human being): Matter, Sensations, Perceptions, Mental Formations and Consciousness are constantly changing; they do not remain the same for two consecutive moments. The Samurai knew that in every moment one is born and one dies. As the Buddha said, *"O Bhikkus every moment you are born, decay and die. Thus, even now during this lifetime, every moment we are born and die, but we continue."*[xxv]

In a series of unbroken changes that continues throughout every moment the Samurai, through their deep Zen practice, were like the analogy of the flame that burns through the night, it is not the same flame nor is it another, the child is not the same as the elder person as the human being transforms through the experiences of the many years. The differences between life and death is only a thought moment: the last thought moment in this life conditions the first through moment in the so called next life, which, in fact, is the continuity of the same series.

It reminds me of the story of the Master trying to teach the student how to shoot an arrow from their bow. *"The right art cried the Master, is purposeless, aimless! The obstinate you trying to learn how to shoot the arrow for the sake of hitting the goal, the less you will succeed in the one and the further the other will recede. What stands in your way is that you have a much too willful will. You think that what you do not do yourself does not happen...by letting go of yourself, leaving yourself and everything yours behind you so decisively that nothing more is left of you but a purposeless tension."*[xxvi]

The Third Sword-Courage has many aspects and sometimes the Samurai needed new challenges to carry them into other directions for further development. They studied and disciplined themselves so that they could assess any crisis in a blink of an eye. They trained so that their true character would be revealed. The courageous choice and challenge arose when the realization dawned about the next opponent...and that was meeting their own self on the road of their fated journey.

(New York City Ken Zen Institute (photo by Nancy Sensei)

*

The test

Meeting oneself is the wakefulness and celebration of the moment. The following remembrance of my examination for a higher degree in Kendo defines wakefulness clearly and happened when I was required to have a match with my *Sensei* Reverend Shunshin Kan. Several students including myself were practicing diligently for this moment. We all knew it was a great honor to spar with *Sensei* Kan even though we knew at the same time he was testing our skill level to either advance us or keep us back for the continuation of our practice.

Less experienced Kendo practitioners always played the more advanced students so that accuracy of movement and mind control would sharpen. The test of one's advancement was always found when matching *Sensei* Kan's skill.

The day came when I was to be tested by the master swordsman, my *Sensei*. I bowed in reverence and gratitude. As we entered *"chudan"* the position called the standard *"kama-e"* where the practitioner can either attack or be attacked, *Sensei's* move was so fast, I did not see it coming. One point was counted and I only had one left. He kept coming at me, I kept blocking to ward off his strikes but his strikes became harder and harder to bear. I thought his blows would kill me. I did my best to try and protect myself but finally due to severe pain, I began to cry and I dropped my *shinai* point to the ground and I backed up. I felt utterly defeated and physically hurt and embarrassed by my emotional outburst.

Sensei Kan, seeing my reaction, quickly moved over to me and grabbed me by my *kendogu* (vest plate armour). He pulled me to him with such a force that our metal masked clinked. He looked deeply into my eyes, piercing through the metal bars of the mask and yelled, *"When are you going to get out of the way."* For a moment, I was bewildered and shocked by his comment. I hung for an eternal instant in an empty place and then an amazing thing happened. I can only describe the moment as a lightening strike illuminating my head from being hit so hard, I saw stars. I knew instantly what I had to do...clarity....space....nothing.

We went back to *"chudan"* and there in the eternal silence my body/sword moved and struck his throat (*tsuki*).... considered the highest point in a Kendo match. I won my advancement and my higher belt at that time. *Sensei* and I bowed to each other to close the match. He congratulated me and I was forever altered by the experience.

I was now at a point in my awareness and skill where I could train others, especially those new members in the graceful art of

Kendo. I have never forgotten that moment with *Sensei* Kan. It was in pure silence and stillness in action that I found the path the Samurai speak of.

"Here it should be noted that the conscious mind gives rise to the ego. The ego is that aspect of the mind that takes the self as the measuring stick of the world and ultimately seeks self-preservation. Hence, it is the ego which breeds fear, frustration and confusion. Under these circumstances the most effective move to make is an all out 'go for broke' attack, which is referred to a "sutemi "(literally 'body- abandoning'). It is in this kind of attack—an attack in which there is no intrusion of the ego-based intellect—that a kendo practitioner is apt to discover Mushin." [xxvii]

(Photograph by Shingeru Tamura of D.T. Suzuki)

While studying with Reverend Kan, he suggested we read the books of D.T. Suzuki who was considered one of the greatest exponents of Zen in the USA. His books became a foundation for contemplative study in the Martial Arts as his understanding of different arising states of consciousness where clearly and precisely articulated especially concerning the meanings of "*Mushin* and *Satori*".

Master Zen writer, Daisetsu Teitaro Suzuki (1870-1966) translated "*Mushin*" as mind of no mind. It is a state of consciousness where the ego directed self is no longer the state that clouds the vision by distractions and fears. Because of his long and arduous meditation practices, studying under his master teacher Soen, a noted Zen master of the day, and under his guidance, Suzuki attained *satori* (which he describes as sudden enlightenment). D. T. Suzuki knew that taming the ego developed concentration and alertness to all surrounding outer circumstances but most importantly that which was arising from within. He worked with Paul Carus and translated many books and articles for him. (e.g. The Discourse on the Awakening of Faith in the Mahayana published 1900; Outline of Mahayana Buddhism published in 1907). He taught in the USA and travelled broadly throughout the European continent bringing Buddhist understanding to Western countries. Master Suzuki was an amazing force that brought clarity and insight to the Western world and giving impulse to many schools of Zen Buddhism that followed after his passing.

*

An Incident after Training

The experience of *Mushin* can come about unexpectedly but when in training which requires careful analysis of the body-mind connection the spirit and intuition will naturally broaden. Therefore the dedicated training that is necessary for the individual is for the purpose of making quick decisions, without fear predicating over the difficult circumstances that arise, these types of decisions can save one's life and others.

Many years later, after training with *Sensei* Reverend Kan, I moved from the East Coast and had an encounter when I was a studying with *Sensei* Kim on the streets of San Francisco. I had already been studying with *Sensei* Kim for several years at this time and I was now teaching Philosophical courses at the University. Practice was very long that day, about four hours and when the class session closed it was nighttime. I did not have a car and I used public transportation. Near the edge of tunnel there was a bus stop that would take me to my apartment. I closed up my gear and started walking to the bus stop above Chinatown near a tunnel entrance that led to downtown. Usually there were many people always around on the streets, but this night was a bit quiet and I did not think much about it and I simply waited patiently for the bus to arrive.

While I was standing there, I put my bag down by my feet and took out a paper with notes on it to see if I could read while I waited. At that very moment, a man jumped from behind me and held a knife to my throat. Being in training for four hours just before this event, I somehow relaxed, I let all my weight slither to the ground like jellyfish, pulling away from his grip and spun on my toes and threw a blow to his knees with the palms of my hands. I heard his knees crack and then he screamed and fell backward on the ground. I knew he would not be able to go anywhere. I left him on the ground and ran quickly to find a phone booth to call the police. I went back to the perpetrator and waited with him until the police came. He was fairly incoherent and I could not get much information out of him.

The police came and after I told them my part of the story, they recognized the fellow who was being loaded into an ambulance. Apparently, he was a user and distributer of heroine and this was not the first time he was known to the police for violent behavior. It was a long night, I had to go to the station and file a report and then try to get home to sleep before I had to teach my morning class for Elder Self Defense and then teach classes at the University in the afternoon and then enter training sessions with *Sensei* Kim in the evening.

It was impossible to sleep or eat. My body was shaking terribly with the whole ordeal. I waited until evening class to tell *Sensei* Kim what transpired. He listened carefully to my story but when I was finished he criticized me thoroughly for not taking a long run to work off the cortisol produced by the adrenal glands activated by the surprise attack. I realized his common sense and knew his criticism was for my health and protection. I began to run regularly until I felt the experience leave my body memory. The added hour of running every evening became a deep meditation for body-mind integration and I kept it up for years as a solitary practice. Through the encounter with the perpetrator, I saw with greater perception the reason why working in a gym with my dojo mates was not only for continuing practice but also for informing muscular memory that arises from daily exercises.

I came to understand while studying with *Sensei* Kim that Martial Arts training are a form of self-therapy. The *Kata*, all levels of "*rondure*"(one to one encounter), the "*kiai*" (which is like a primal scream), brings one into a reality that is met with courage, which does not filter out the intellect or emotions but encompasses them in new way. One develops an experiential knowledge-a knowledge learned by intuitive feeling, a somatic learning, if you will. A Martial Artist has to know their body thoroughly thus the reason for daily practice. When the knowledge of the body is truly gained, one is able to control every muscle and sometimes even the involuntary ones. Therefore, *Sensei* Kim was constantly bringing us back to the *Kata,* and urged us all to sit *Zazen.*

The Martial Artist has to finally ask himself/herself, what is *Satori*? What is *Nirvana*? Volumes have been written to try to explain these states of consciousness but somehow through intellectual explanation it seems to confuse the mind as the human language lacks in detailing the perfection of an ultimate reality where courage is born. It is understood that the human language centers mostly on what the sense organs and mental descriptions offer rather than the super mundane experiences, which is in another category then what, we would term, Truth. Therefore it is difficult to find words to describe the indescribable.

There is a story about a fish and a tortoise that expresses this language difficulty.

Two friends were talking to each other; the fish that has no words in his vocabulary to express the nature of the solid land was talking to his friend the tortoise. The tortoise told his friend the fish that he just returned to the lake after walking on the land. 'Of course' the fish said, 'You mean swimming?' The tortoise tried to explain that one could not swim on the land as it was solid, and that one walked on it. But the fish insisted that there could be nothing like that, that it must be liquid like his lake, with waves, and that one must be able to dive and swim there. [xxviii]

The Third Sword-Courage, which the Samurai exhibited, had valuable insights that proved to be beneficial to the evolution of human consciousness. The human body is an instrument in tune with the universal vibrations that permeate space and time. It is a mechanism of highly qualified and synthesized energy that can replicate what is necessary for the personal as well as the collective manifestation necessary for the evolution of the species.

The Samurai were attuned to the need of their personal development as well as the need of the community. There was always a conflict of these two principles and to solve the seemingly oppositional aspects the Samurai turned to The Bushido Code. Because a moral code can be seen as arbitrary, sometimes too rigid for the unpredictable challenges arising in life, the Samurai often turned to a noble individualism and a supreme inner evocation of spiritual law born from disciplined practice, insight, intuition, and fearless association with all beings. Their direct philosophical expression and contribution to the world was absolute freedom born from their inner life.

These beings were not lawless Ronin's who were out in the community whacking someone for payment paid to them by gang bosses who held vendettas as the movies and media portrays. It is here, that we enter the stories of Yoshida Kotaro, (below), whose discipline gives evidence to his effective mastery that unmasked all that opposed the practice of *Mushin* (empty mind). His conscious realization turned inward and it was this level of courageous mastery that *Sensei* Kim honored and communicated his story to us.

There was always great difficulty for the Samurai to hold their sacred task of going inward and oppose the conventional behavior of the society. To go inward meant to enter into the darkest void as the firm support of the mundane, or common reality fell away. The Samurai preferred to enter into the extraordinary that assured a strict reliance on the fundamental reality that birthed itself through discipline, conscious awakened mind and a trust in their intuition.

(Photograph by Kristin Fein)

*

Yoshida Kotaro

Sensei Kim spoke a great deal about the unusual Samurai, Yoshida because he met him in person in 1953. He praised Yoshida's special psychic development especially due to the fact he was under the instructions of his Master teacher, Takeda Sokaku who taught him principles rather than techniques. Sokaku helped him develop breath techniques and methods to control his consciousness and methods to use his intuition and psychic abilities. Sokaku felt that techniques only worked under certain circumstances whereas a principle can be applied to many different solutions.

Over the years and under the watchful eye of Sokaku, Yoshida developed a powerful "*Ki*" energy that could move objects. For example, when *Sensei* Kim was working out with barbells with Yoshida present in the room, Sensei Kim's mother-in-law walked into the gym. *Sensei* Kim said he lost concentration just for a moment and dropped the heavy barbell. But before it reached the floor, Yoshida's concentration suspended the barbells from touching the ground and stayed in mid air. Although this was almost impossible to believe, there were now other witnesses to Yoshida's great psychic ability.

Yoshida began developing these psychic skills well before his eighteenth birthday. He believed that through relaxation when there is no tension in the muscles, that one could find pure strength when needed. He often spoke of the breath and how one can imagine the breath settling down into the *tanden* (solar plexus) and that any excess breath goes down to the big toe. Then when the Martial Artist strikes, at the moment of impact one explodes, relaxing instantly after the action takes place. He realized that a Martial Artist must learn relaxation and softness above all and then learn how to burst out in an explosive force. He indicated that when one is tense the subconscious mind would not function. He therefore recommended that one meet all circumstances with neutral mind.

He used this principle of relaxation in *Kata* practice while he was training in the mountains. During his training period, the mountain regions were filled with bandits who always wanted to terrorize the sheepherders and farmers. While he was staying with a farmer who generously gave him room and board because Yoshida got rid of a raider bandit who was causing enormous trouble for the farmer, Yoshida had the following experiences.

*

Yoshida and the Bandits

When the gang of bandits heard what Yoshida had done to one of their gang members, they wanted to raid the farm, kill everyone and loot the place. Yoshida knew, through his psychic ability, that

63

the vendetta would occur sooner than later. So he prepared the entrance to the farmhouse by removing the floorboards right at the entrance of the front door.

There were fourteen members of the bandit gang that came one night to attack the farmer. Yoshida left the front door open. The gang leader decided to send in one of the bandits every three minutes. Each one entered the door, one after another. There was no fighting, no voice only a swish sound could be heard as Yoshida removed the head of the bandit as he was waiting at the side of the door entrance. Finally, only five of the attacking gang members were left. Yoshida put on the clothing of the sub leader and went outside and with a quick cut of his sword killed all three in one move, the other two ran away and told the story of his skill to everyone and this story became legend.

*

Yoshida and the Mosquitos

Yoshida also experimented with herbs and chemicals. He went to a mosquito-infested area half naked where he was attached by thousands of mosquitos that in their frenzy bit him all over his face and body. Instantly, they all fell down dead. This happened because Yoshida was taking arsenic and he wanted to see if it had an effect on his blood without killing him.

*

Yoshida and the Boulders

He would also experiment with moving large boulders from a distance without ever touching them. He stood in a position similar to that of one in the *Kata style* (soft form) movements with his palms facing out straight from his chest. When he moved his palms forward very slowly and consciously, the boulders moved the same equal distance. [xxix]

The Samurai's most honored virtue was their courage. It was a telling excellence of their training and dedicated discipline. What is respected about courage is the fact that often some kind of act of self-sacrifice follows an act of unselfish motivation. Because the Samurai trained their minds in Zen principles they prepared their temperaments to be more neutral when facing harsh unexpected circumstances. What we have here is a training strategy that brings into play a moral responsibility.

"Whereas courage is always respected from a psychological or sociological standpoint, it is only really morally estimable when at least partially in the service of others and more or less free of immediate self-interest." [xxx]

Courage for the Samurai showed a low degree of fear due to their willingness to die in an action that was either in defense of their lives when others attacked them. They would rather die in a battle with an enemy, than plead for their lives as the story of Yoshida indicates when he was taken prisoner by the Manchurian bandits.

*

Yoshida taken as prisoner by the Manchurian Bandits

When Yoshida was about 33 years old, Manchurian bandits captured him. Accompanying him was another Japanese man who worked for the Manchurian railway as a spy as did many of the other workers. The bandits observed Yoshida's long stick but they did not notice the small knife he hid in his waistband.

While talking to one of his captors, Yoshida mentioned that he was not a spy and he would not be coerced into being one. *"That is too bad"*, said his captor, *"as the Manchurians always killed their prisoners."* Yoshida took this news calmly and he continued to carefully observe the Manchurians and became familiar with their manners and customs. He spoke to the head bandit and offered a challenge with anyone they would match against him. If he won, he wanted his freedom. The bandits accepted his proposal and thought it would be great entertainment for the bandits, as surely Yoshida would die. They then sent to China for an expert in the double broadsword.

Yoshida only had a week to prepare for the match and remained under difficult circumstances. He was not allowed to use any sword against the expert but they said he could use his long stick. When the Chinese swordsman arrived, Yoshida watched him practice. Yoshida tried to come up with a defense so that he could prepare himself against him. This rehearsal in his mind did not seem to satisfy him. He felt that he must finally go into the ultimate physical and mental act of *"mushin"*, (empty mind), the true essence of meditation. He knew he had to be entirely in the moment as he could die anytime. Yoshida realized he needed to think of death as his friend.

When the time for the match came, Yoshida stood calmly outside of the experts reach with his stick in his left hand. As the expert came down on Yoshida's head with one of his swords, Yoshida slightly parried and lunged with concentrated force, penetrating his stick into the solar plexus of the experts belly. He then twisted the stick for a deathblow and jumped into *"Gedan Kama-e"* (the practitioner can attack or receive an attack). The expert was dead and Yoshida was freed from the prison. [xxxi]

Brave men act, write Aristotle, *"for honors sake,"* which can also be stated as *"for beauty of the courageous action."* Or *"for the love of good."* (Nicomachean Ethics, III, 8.) *"Now, the courageous man always keeps his presence of mind (so far as man can). So though he will fear these fearful things, he will endure them as he ought and as reason bid him, the sake of that which is noble; for this is the aim of virtue."* [xxxii]

Courage under these extraordinary circumstances is not the absence of fear entirely, but rather the ability to confront and overcome fear that might reasonably exist. Courage is a willingness to act usually under unforeseen circumstances. It is a decision that arises quickly and without trepidation that allows fear to govern the mind and senses. Courage can be understood as a refusal to submit to anything but the Truth of the experience what arises in the discovery of the moment.

There is an offering in the schools of philosophy such as indicated by Comte-Sponville, where he states, *" Reason is in every instance universal and anonymous, whereas courage is always singular and personal. And if we sometimes need courage to think, just as we need to suffer or fight, it is because no one can think for us—or suffer or fight for us—and because reason, or truth, is insufficient and cannot spare us the task of overcoming whatever it is within us that wavers and resists, that would prefer a comforting illusion or a convenient lie. Whence what we call intellectual courage, the refusal to let fear govern the life of the mind, the refusal to submit to anything but the truth, which fears nothing even if it is itself freighting."* [xxxiii]

For Yoshida, courage was knowledge and this was the reason why he was highly observant in all manner of things and situations. He based his philosophy on inner vibrations which he called his *"cosmic circle,"* that was articulated to his students in his Eight Points of preparation and development:

1. **One receives visions usually through meditation practice, one's limited consciousness of reality, from that point, ceases.**
2. **One senses there exists a greater power than oneself; at that point your world ceases.**
3. **The person becomes One with that power, and then you cease.**
4. **One passes into a void, you pass the Divine and the Divine ceases.**
5. **One has nothing to lose in this life if you do not fear death.**
6. **Everyone has a cosmic circle based on his or her inner vibrations and that is where you receive spiritual sustenance.**
7. **One must find their cosmic vibration within themselves; a teacher is only a guide.**
8. **Know your body and learn how to control it.**

CHAPTER FOUR

The Core of the Samurai

A Perspective on the Battle of Life

When we regard our life, we look at the many levels and aspects of those activities that occupied us. We might have looked at the positive and negative qualities that emerged into our consciousness that directed us into deeper contemplation or confused us by keeping our purpose obscured from our intuitive ways of knowing our situation and ourselves. Whatever profession we might have developed over the many years, if one lacks the knowledge of how to battle with life; one misses the deep benefit from life's purpose.

So, one might ask what is the battle of life and what do we have to learn? The first important piece of knowledge is the skill of the fight and the second is the skill of how to make peace. War and peace come from the same source and have their place in the evolution of societies. However, if our limited understanding does not comprehend what civilizations have gone through over the millennia one's knowledge of the evolution of humanity will only take sides and not see the eventual turning inward that delivers us from ignorance. The more we go inward in our journey of exploring ourselves, the fuller realities can be grasped so that the knowledge of the battle of life and peace can be won.

We battle with our consciousness to help us find peace with our spiritual purpose. The Samurai knew that their journey was not as individual as one might perceive but rather of the world's movement as an individual's body, mind and spirit form the whole universe and the evolution of the universe is in the realization of the individual's consciousness. It is said in the mystical writings of the Sufi masters, *"An individual's life can fill the gap between the dawn of creation and the last day. A human being does not realize how important is their life, their state of 'self'; and the study of their own life and their own self is a study of the greatest importance."* [xxxiv]

One's evolution is key to infinite possibilities pressing against oppositional aspects of life. For example, light comes from friction showing two forces sticking against each other that power, knowledge and life are then created. In the Holy Qur'an it is indicated that the world was created out of darkness, giving evidence that wisdom comes out of ignorance. Our ignorance binds us to certain attachments that arise in our personality such as: the stuff of being and wanting a constant state of satisfaction and happiness, a struggle with our passions and emotions and our struggle with inertia and negligence.

As discipline evolves in one's nature, one begins to sense the origin and the goal of the variety of personalities. It is revealed to the observant practitioner how dualism arising from misconstrued concepts and misguided judgments that bring us into opposition with one another. Where there is plurality there must be conflict; although conflict seems a tragedy, the true tragedy is ignorance. The Samurai attempted to conquer these dualisms by holding their courageous attitudes that impressed upon them their reasons for continuing their disciplines and training. Their training taught them when to retreat or advance without the intoxication of the ego motivating their actions.

*

Be like a mirror

One afternoon after practice, *Sensei* Kim offered us a special lecture that he called, *"Be like a mirror"*. He began his lecture by indicating whomever laid down the precepts of the Martial Arts philosophy must have realized that a human being who attains *"Mushin"* (empty mind) was able to clearly see the stoppages in the mental realm. What I believe he meant by that comment was concerning how a person navigates between the infinite array of thoughts that rise and fall in the mind sometimes as opinions, judgments, movements or an action of some kind.

When one would face a Samurai in a fight to the death, the Samurai just waited for the person to become frightened or distracted by a thought, and when the person did become frightened, there would be a stoppage in one's mental realm at which time the Samurai would strike. In other words the Samurai would attack during the opponents blind spot when the thoughts where shifting. Even if an opponent was thinking, *'I am going to do this, or I am going to try this move,*' in between these thoughts there are small distracted moments, although they might only be a split second, it opens the door to the opponents defeat.

If one remains calm and does not think, then you will be like a mirror, you will pick up everything and reflect accurately on what is being reflected on your mirror, but if one gets caught in the shifting sea of thoughts, it opens the door to attack. Because the Samurai have trained themselves to accept death, their minds are like mirrors, as they do not reflect opinions, judgments or thoughts. The mirror does not favor any particular image arising in the mental realm. The mirror is neutral. Very few people could reach that level, but when they do, one cannot be attacked even from behind. Thus the Samurai were formidable opponents. [xxxv]

*

The step into Bushido

The disciplines that were self-imposed by the Samurai have nothing to do with a religious or moral convergence predicated by dread or punishments that might have descended through conventional religious doctrines. Fear often gave the general population reasons for ones hope and desire to be fulfilled. At the same time, shining a light on the dread of punishment as a restriction concerning any action toward others that would be cruel or motivated by hatred brought the Samurai into unbalanced moral action unacceptable in Bushido philosophy. Actions that were virtuous incite human beings toward the hope of reward, which bribes one into acceptance of religious protocol. Righteousness is then the safest policy and virtue the best overseer. The Bushido Code offered the Samurai a reverse level of discrimination as they gave preference to the inner code of *"Mushin"* (empty mind).

When a person is assured that the wicked will pay and be defeated by the good and the worthy, the general populace falls into line. Although the law of cause and effect is a truth that cannot be ignored, and karma is infallible, most human beings need some kind of enforced guideline to turn the inner nature toward a diplomatic compromise between the egotistic demand of getting what one wants from the world to a larger perspective which recognizes oneself and the community as a united whole. A marriage, therefore, of convenience between what is virtuous and right not only for oneself but also for what abides in the fundamental collective is an individual law of conduct that matures over time.

The one who is trained in a higher ideal, as the Samurai, where the higher law of the spirit abides and who can accept with equanimity the evolution of one's life without egotistic motivation are the trained practitioners of the Martial Arts. These are the ones who instilled self-knowledge, control and moral strength through the disciplined practice of the mind, body and spirit.

The Samurai's ethics were realized from a certain perspective, as they did not follow fixed rules of conduct that governed the populace. They rather followed the principles that formed the Seven Bushido Codes: **No parents only heaven and earth; No home, only the bass of the spine; No life or death only breath; No laws only adaptation; No principles only self; No talent only wit; No sword only *Mushin*.** The Seven Bushido Codes motivated the inner conditions of clear spiritual consciousness. When higher consciousness activated from these seven principles determined all interactions the Samurai sought practice above all else.

The Samurai therefore embodied the necessary self-control and restraint in order to discipline their minds through their physical training. As they liberated themselves from conventional reactivity through fear-based impulses, the Bushido Code placed before them obligations that often brought vital success as their actions revealed skill, control and mental tranquility. These actions by the Samurai grew into an empirical basis for the Bushido Code to take hold as a philosophical path.

But it must be said that the larger ideal of the Samurai is not an absolute. If what they followed were simply blind obedience to outward moral law through a code of conduct only, the narrowness of a rigid moral code would kill the higher law of the Samurai's spirit, which was attempting to rise above the impermanent laws of the land and politics of the time. The restriction of the ruling powers that tyrannized the populous neglected the creative flexibilities necessary for the transformation of consciousness. Here is where the Samurai contributed great moral significance to society as their insistence of following the inner disciplines rather than outward rigid obedience to the imposition of imperfect laws of moral conduct, the Samurai became living examples of the intuitive codes that evolved from moment to moment spontaneously.

No outer form or mechanical rule can aid in the evolution of the creative inner state of the Samurai. The answer comes from the inner being and their discovery of what can be revealed by their self-fulfillment when their actions abide by the true act of justice, truth and sacrifice. For they must finally, in the moment of clarity and emptiness, acknowledge and bow down to the greatness that only belongs to the infinite.

Any retardation in their skill and growth, any mental action that took them backwards from the flowering of their courage, purity, strength and self-giving was an unacceptable punishment that tarnished their luminous striving for their calm state of equanimity. The real Samurai, not the 'want-a-be' Samurai, were those extraordinary beings who accepted the pain, sufferings and difficulties of life. All the challenges of those who wanted to measure their own skill against the truly accomplished master Samurai because people innately sensed that these unique practitioners lifted themselves above the belt of the tightening empire of restriction. They recognized that all pain is an opportunity for growth. Here, is where the Samurai found the good fortune for outer success and internal liberation that was immediately transformed into the Bushido Code that addresses having Heaven and Earth as one's parents and the *Tanden* (Solar Plexus) as their only home.

(Photograph by Robin J. Laflamme)

*

The Long Discourse of the Buddha

It is noteworthy to regard the teachings of the Buddha given in the Long Discourse (*Digha Nikaya*) in the *Samannaphala Sutta* (The Fruits of the Homeless Life) where he gives evidence to major considerations of training mind and body as a pathway to liberation. It is given that the Samurai knew and studied these lectures with carefulness and consideration although many did not take the path of the monk, the Samurai new the fruit of the homeless life.

V. 85, *"And he, with mind concentrated...having gained imperturbability, applies and directs his mind to the production of a mind-made body. And out of this body he produces another body, having a form, mind-made, complete in all its limbs and faculties".*

V. 86, "*It is just as if a man were to draw out a reed from its sheath. He might think: 'This is the reed, this is the sheath, reed and sheath are different. Now the reed had been pulled from the sheath.' Or, as if a man were to draw a sword from the scabbard. He might think: 'this is the sword, this is the scabbard, sword and scabbard are different. Now the sword has been drawn from the scabbard.' Or, as if a man were to draw a snake from its (old) skin. He might think: 'this is the snake, this is the skin, snake and skin are different. Now the snake has been drawn from its skin.' In the same way a monk with mind concentrated...directs his mind to the production of a mind-made body. He draws out of this body having form, mind-made, complete with all its limbs and faculties. This is a fruit of the homeless life more excellent and perfect than the former ones.*"

V. 87, "*And he, with a mind concentrated...applies and directs his mind to the various supernormal powers. He then enjoys different powers: being one, he becomes many – being many, he becomes one; he appears and disappears; he passes through fences, walls and mountains unhindered as if through air; he sinks into the ground and emerges from it as if it were water; he walks on the water without breaking the surface as if on land; he flies cross-legged through the sky like a bird with wings; he even touches and strokes with his hand the sun and moon, mighty and powerful as they are; and he travels in the body as far as the Brahma world.*"

V. 91, "*And he, with mind concentrated...applies and directs his mind to the knowledge of others' minds. He knows and distinguishes with his mind the minds of other beings or other persons. He knows the mind with passion to be with passion; he knows the mind without passion to be without passion; he knows the mind with hate to be with hate; he knows the mind without hate to be without hate. He knows the deluded mind to be deluded; he knows the undeluded mind to be undeluded. He knows the narrow mind to be narrow; he knows the broad mind to be broad. He knows the expanded mind to be expanded;*"

he knows the unexpanded mind to be unexpanded. He knows the surpassed mind to be surpassed; he knows the unsurpassed mind to be unsurpassed. He knows the concentrated mind to be concentrated; he knows the unconcentrated mind to be unconcentrated. He knows the liberated mind to be liberated; he knows the unliberated mind to be unliberated."

V. 96, "It is just as if there were a lofty building at a crossroads, and man with good eyesight standing there might see people entering or leaving a house, walking in the street, or sitting in the middle of the crossroads. And he might think: 'These are entering a house...' Just so, with the divine eye...he sees beings passing away and rearising...this is the fruit of the homeless life."

V. 97, "And he with mind concentrated, purified and cleansed, unblemished, free from impurities, malleable, workable, established and having gained imperturbability, applies and directs his mind to the knowledge of the destruction of the corruptions. He knows as it really is: 'this is the origin of suffering,' he knows as it really is: 'This is the cessation of suffering.' And he knows as it really is: 'these are the corruptions', this is the origin of the corruptions', this the cessation of the corruptions', This is the path leading to the cessation of the corruptions. And through his knowing and seeing his mind is delivered from the corruption of sense-desire, from the corruption of becoming, from the corruption of ignorance, and the knowledge arises in him: 'this is deliverance!', and he knows: 'Birth is finished, the holy life has been led, done is what had to be done, there is nothing further here."

V. 98, "Just as if, Sire, in the midst of the mountains there were a pond, clear as a polished mirror, where a man with good eyesight standing on the bank could see oyster-shells, gravel banks, and shoals of fish, on the move or stationary. And he might think: 'This pond is clear...there are oyster-shells...' just so, with mind concentrated...he knows: 'Birth is finished, the holy life has been led, done is what had to be done, homeless life, visible here and now, which is more excellent and perfect than the previous fruits. And, Sire, there is no fruit of the homeless life, visible here and now, that is more excellent and perfect than this."[xxxvi]

The path of the Martial Artist is not for the timid. One is called to face life and death with equanimity and strength of character as elicited in the accomplishments of the Masters presented in these previous chapters.

Odagiri Ichiun found Satori through the *Kata;* **Hariya Sekiun** revealed how to marshal his inner power; **Gichin Funakoshi** brought the philosophy of inner control by never striking first; **Terada Soyu** read the minds of his opponents through "old school techniques"; **Kyan Chotoku** developed inner sensitivity so that he could activate *"Ki"* instantaneously; **Yagyu** was master swordsman and an accomplished artist of Ikebana and was able to intuitively perceive the outcome of warrior clans; **Yoshida Kotaro** whose sacred task was to develop inward concentration which brought methods for developing intuition and the natural *"Ki"* existing in every individual. **Jack Seito-san** was a *Kata* and meditation master; **Reverend Kan** whose journey of transformation formed a school of Kendo and Iaido training for Martial Artists Internationally; **Sensei Kim** became a prodigious teacher of thousands of students by offering history, philosophy, Bushido principles and methods of the Samurai to his pupils

If one who studies in the Martial Arts is irresistibly driven towards their goal, and they commit to a path of concerted discipline and training the person will self-reveal and unwrap fear-based behavior. The individual must have the courage to leap into the Truth of their inner state and become united with it. There can be no reservation to take the lowly road of the student or beginner who is willing to learn. One who can become open to receiving new insights that transform one's consciousness will inevitably be led to spiritual freedom and this is truly blessed because everything changes by the way we look at it.

If the Martial Artist survives the horrors of their inner nightmares and begins to look face to face at the unbroken truth of who they really are without inner repulsion or desire to back up and weaken the resolve to go forward, then one's higher destiny will be accomplished. Then and only then, one is inevitably brought to the Infinite Origin from which we all come from and from this Origin is brought back into life again.

References

Aristotle. (2005). *Nicomachean Ethics*. New York: Barnes & Noble Books.

Benedict, Ruth. (1959). *The Chrysanthemum and the Sword-Patterns of Japanese Culture*. Rutland, Vermont and Tokyo: Charles E. Tuttle Co.

Comte-Sponville, André. (1996). *A Small Treatise of the Great Virtues*. New York: A Metropolitan Owl Book.

Draeger, Sonn and Smith, Robert, W. (1969). *Asian Fighting Arts*. Tokyo: Kodansha International.

Embree, John, F. (1945). *The Japanese Nation*. New York: Farrar Rinehart.

Fonsdal, Gil. (2006). *Dhammapada-A New Translation of the Buddhist Classic with Annotations*. Boston and London: Shambhala.

Gluck, Jay. (1962). *Zen Combat,* New York: Ballantine Books.

Haines, Bruce, A. (1968). *Karate's History and Traditions.* Rutland, Vermont and Tokyo: Charles E. Tuttle Company.

Herrigel, Eugen. (Tr. R.F.C. Hull), (1953). *Zen in the Art of Archery.* New York: Vintage Books.

Junzo, Sasamori and Gordon. (1964, 1974). *This is Kendo-The Art of Japanese Fencing.* Rutland Vermont and Tokyo: Charles E. Tuttle Company.

Kant, Immanuel. (Tr. James W. Erlington). (1964). *The Metaphysical Principles of Virtue (Part 2 of the Metaphysics of Morals,).* Library of Liberal Arts, Bobbs-Merrill.

Khan, Hazrat Inayat. (1978). *Sufi Message Vol. VI, The Alchemy of Happiness.* Katwijk, Holland: Servire Publications.

Kerr, George H. (1974, 2018). *Okinawa: A History of an Island People.* Tokyo: Tuttle Publishing Company.

Kim, Richard. (1974). *The Weaponless Warriors-An Informal History of Okinawan Karate.* Los Angeles: Ohara Publications.

Kiyota, Minoru. (1995). *Kendo and Its Philosophy, History and Means to Personal Growth.* London and New York: Kegan Paul International.

Legge, James (Tr.). (1991). *Confucian Analects.* Taipei: SMC Publishing Inc.

Musashi, Miyamoto. (Tr. from Japanese by Victor Harris). (1974). *The Classic Guide to Strategy* Woodstock, New York: Overlook Press.

Nitobe, Inazo. (1905). *Bushido: The Soul of Japan.* New York: G.P. Putnam's & Son.

Nukariya, Kaiten. (1973). *The Religion of the Samurai*. London: Luzac & Company, LTD.

Rahula, Walpola. (1959, 1974). *What the Buddha Taught*. New York: Grove Weidenfeld.

Santena, Peter Della. (1997). *The Tree of Enlightenment: An Introduction to the Major Traditions of Buddhism*. Taipei, Taiwan: The Corporate Body of the Buddha Educations Foundation.

Suzuki, D.T. (1944). *Studies in Zen-Interpretation of the Zen Experience*. "East & West". (Ed. Dr. Charles A. Moore), Princeton, New Jersey: Princeton University Press.

----------*The Field of Zen* (1969, 1970). (Ed. Christmas Humphreys), New York, Evanston, London: Perennial Library.

----------*Zen and Japanese Culture*. (1959). New York: Pantheon.

----------*Manual of Zen Buddhism*. (1960). New York: Grove Press.

Tohei, Koichi. (1966, 1975). *Aikido in Daily Life*. Tokyo: Rikugel Publishing House.

Venerable Nanamoli (Tr). (1960). *Paramatthajolika Commentary*. Pali Text Society.

Walshe, Maurice. (Tr.) *Thus Have I Heard-The Long Discourses of the Buddha (Digha Nikaya)*. London: Wisdom Publications, 1987.

Warner, Gordon. "An Old Sword flashes in the Dark Shadow". *Black Belt Magazine*, Vol. 1, No. 3, Los Angeles, CA, April 1962.

----------Bushido, "Misused and Misunderstood", *Kashu Minichi*, Los Angeles, CA., December 1959.

----------"Swords and Armor of Europe and Japan". *Black Belt Magazine*, Vol. 1, No. 2., Los Angeles, CA. January 1962.

Watts, Alan. (1999). *The Way of Zen*. New York: Knopf Doubleday Publishing Group.

Yumoto, John, M. (2008). *The Samurai Sword-A Handbook*. Rutland, Vermont: Charles E. Tuttle Co., Inc.

*

<u>End Notes</u>

[i] Miyamoto Mushashi. The Book of Five Rings. The Classic Guide to Strategy (Tr. From Japanese by Victor Harris) Overlook Press, Woodstock, NY : 1974, Pgs. 6 & 7

[ii] Confucian Analects with translation by James Legge. Taipei : SMC Publishing Inc. 1991. P. 139

[iii] Richard Kim, The Weaponless Warriors, An Informal History of Okinawan Karate. Ohara Publications, Incorporated. Los Angeles, CA. : 1974, Pgs. 106 & 107.

[iv] Eugen Herrigel, (Trans. R.F.C. Hull). Zen in the Art of Archery. New York : Vintage Books. 1953, 1971. P. 49.

[v] Sensai Kim's Lecture given October 31st, 1971 at the YWCA-Chinatown, San Francisco.

[vi] Sensai Kim's Lecture on Philosophy of the Samurai given May 25th 1974.

[vii] Sensai Kim's Lecture, May 25th, 1974.

[viii] Sensai Kim's Lecture June 27th 1973.

[ix] Richard Kim. The Weaponless Warriors. Los Angeles, California : Ohara Publications, Inc. 1974. P. 108.

[x] Yin and Yang are principles established from ancient Chinese Philosophy indicating opposing universal energies that compliment each other and are interdependent.

xi Koichi Tohei. Aikido in Daily Life. Tokyo : Rikugei Publishing House, 1966, 1975. P. 87.

xii Sensai Kim's Lecture on Kyan Kiyatake Chotoku.

xiii Myomoto Musashi, Book of Five Rings, Woodstock, New York : The Overland Press, 1974. P. 95

xiv James Legge. (Tr.)The Chinese Classics. Taipei: SMC Publishing Inc. 1991. P. 151.

xv Junzo Sasamori and Gordon Warner. This is Kendo-The Art of Japanese Fencing. Rutland, Vermont & Tokoyo, Japan: Charles E. Tuttle Company, 1964, 1974. P. 34.

xvi Sensai Kim's Lecture February 3, 1974 on Terada Soyu.

xvii Sensai Kim's Lecture March 17th 1973 on Mushashi, Yaghu and Yamaoka Tesshu.

xviii Jack Seito-san sharing his perspective with me during a sitting session in Golden Gate Park, San Francisco, 1973.

xix Walpola Rahula. What the Buddha Taught. New York : Grove Weidenfeld. 1959, 1974. Pgs. 32, 33.

xx Sensai Kim's Lecture on Meditation January 22, 1972.

xxi Gil Fronsdal. Dhammapada-A New Translation of the Buddhist Classic with Annotations. Boston & London : Shambhala, 2006.

xxii Eugen Herrigel. Zen in the Art of Archery. New York : Vintage Books, 1953, 1971. P. 89.

xxiii Sensai Kim's Lecture notes for September 4th 1971.

xxiv Aristotle. Nichomachean Ethics. New York : Barnes & Noble Books, 2005. P. 58.

xxv Quoted from the Paramatthajotika Commentary of the Buddha's own words from the Sutta Nipata (Ultimate Sense), in the Khuddaka Nikaya-part of the Pali Canon of Theravada Buddhism. (Translated by Venerable Nanamoli. Pali Text Society Edition 1960.

xxvi Eugen Herrigel. Zen in the Art of Archery. New York: Random House, 1953, 1971. Pgs. 34, 35.

xxvii Minoru Kiyota. Kendo-Its Philosophy, History and Means to Personal Growth. London & New York : Kegan Paul International, 1995, P. 2.

xxviii Walpola Rahula. What the Buddha Taught. New York: Grove Weidenfeld, 1959, 1974. P. 35.

xxix The Yoshida Stories are extracted from five different lectures that Sensai Kim offered between the months of February 27, 1971 through March 30, 1971.

xxx Comte-Sponville. A Small Treatise on the Great Virtues. New York : Metropolitan Owl Book, 1996, P. 47.

xxxi Sensai Kim's Lecture on Yoshida March 12, 1971.

xxxii Aristotle. Nicomachean Ethics. New York: Barnes & Noble Books, 2005. P. 58.

xxxiii Comte-Sponville. A Small Treatise on the Great Virtues. New York : Metropolitan/Owl Book, 1996. P. 52.

[xxxiv] Hazrat Inayat Khan. The Sufi Message Vol. VI, The Alchemy of Happiness. Katwijk, Holland : Servire Publishers, 1978. P. 78.

[xxxv] Sensai Kim's Lecture notes, November 1973.

[xxxvi] Walshe, Maurice (Trans). Thus Have I Heard-the Long Discourses of the Buddha (Digha Nikaya). London: Wisdom Publications, 1987. Pgs. 104-108.